"*Cognitive Behavioral Therapy for Anxiety* by Mark Fefergrad and Peggy M. A. Richter is a concise primer for therapists interested in learning powerful concepts and techniques for the treatment of anxiety. This is an excellent resource for those beginning their training in CBT."

—**Robert L. Leahy, PhD**, Director,
American Institute for Cognitive Therapy;
Clinical Professor of Psychology,
Weill Cornell Medical College

Cognitive Behavioral Therapy for Anxiety

A NORTON PROFESSIONAL BOOK

Cognitive Behavioral Therapy for Anxiety

Mark Fefergrad
Peggy M. A. Richter

SERIES EDITORS: Paula Ravitz and Robert Maunder

W. W. NORTON & COMPANY

New York | London

7-Column Thought Record used with permission; © 1983 Christine A. Padesky, PhD.
Copyright © 2013 by Mark Fefergrad, Peggy Richter, Paula Ravitz, and Robert Maunder

For information about permission to reproduce selections from this book, write to
Permissions, W. W. Norton & Company, Inc., 500 Fifth Avenue, New York, NY 10110

For information about special discounts for bulk purchases, please contact W. W. Norton
Special Sales at specialsales@wwnorton.com or 800-233-4830

Manufacturing by Quad Graphics
Book design by Kristina Kachele Design, llc
Production manager: Leeann Graham

Library of Congress Cataloging-in-Publication Data
Fefergrad, Mark.
Cognitive behavioral therapy for anxiety / Mark Fefergrad, Peggy Richter.
pages cm. — (Psychotherapy essentials to go)
"A Norton Professional Book."
Includes bibliographical references.
ISBN 978-0-393-70827-1 (pbk.)
1. Anxiety disorders—Treatment—Handbooks, manuals, etc. 2. Cognitive therapy—
Handbooks, manuals, etc. 3. Anxiety. I. Richter, Peggy (Margaret A.) II. Title.
RC531.F45 2013
616.85'220651—dc23

2013007923

ISBN: 978-0-393-70827-1 (pbk.)

W. W. Norton & Company, Inc., 500 Fifth Avenue, New York, N.Y. 10110
www.wwnorton.com
W. W. Norton & Company Ltd., Castle House, 75/76 Wells Street, London W1T 3QT

1 2 3 4 5 6 7 8 9 0

Mark Fefergrad

Thank you very much to all my patients and teachers who have educated me over the years. Even greater thanks to my wonderful, beautiful, devoted, and caring wife, whose support and love have been without boundary.

Peggy Richter

To my father, Max Richter, who inspired in me a love of teaching and the joy that comes from helping others learn.

Mark Fefergrad, MD, MEd, is Assistant Professor and the Director of Postgraduate Education in the Department of Psychiatry at the University of Toronto. He has held several leadership roles with respect to CBT education and is the head of Cognitive Behavioral Therapy at Sunnybrook Health Sciences Centre.

Margaret A. (Peggy) Richter, MD, is the inaugural head of the Frederick W. Thompson Anxiety Disorders Centre at Sunnybrook Health Sciences Centre, focused on research and treatment of obsessive-compulsive disorder (OCD) and related conditions. She is also Associate Professor of Psychiatry at the University of Toronto, a scientist with the Brain Sciences Research Program at Sunnybrook Research Institute, and with the Neurogenetics Section, Neurosciences Department, at the Centre for Addiction and Mental Health.

Paula Ravitz, MD, is Associate Professor, Morgan Firestone Psychotherapy Chair, and Associate Director of the Psychotherapy, Health Humanities, and Education Scholarship Division for the Department of Psychiatry at the University of Toronto, where she leads IPT training. She is also the director of the Mt. Sinai Psychotherapy Institute. Her clinical practice, teaching, and research focus on IPT and attachment-informed psychotherapy.

Robert Maunder, MD, is Associate Professor in the Department of Psychiatry at the University of Toronto and head of research for Mount Sinai Hospital's Department of Psychiatry. His primary research interest is the role of interpersonal attachment on health.

Contents

Acknowledgments

Producing *Psychotherapy Essentials to Go* has depended on and benefited from the support and expertise of many people. We wish to acknowledge and thank Aaron T. Beck and Christine Padesky, the developers of Cognitive Behavioral Therapy, who, with others, have built the foundation from which this treatment has grown. We are grateful to the contributing authors whose hard work, wisdom, and creativity as educators and clinicians are represented; the Ontario Ministry of Health and Long Term Care, who provided funding to the educational outreach pilot project team of the Northern Psychiatric Outreach Program at the Centre for Addiction and Mental Health (CAMH); Nancy McNaughton and the University of Toronto Standardized Patient Program; Robert Swenson and the Ontario Psychiatric Outreach Program; the University of Toronto Department of Psychiatry; the Mount Sinai Hospital

Department of Psychiatry; Molyn Leszcz and the Morgan Firestone Psychotherapy Chair; Scott Mitchell; the Canadian Mental Health Association's northern Ontario branch executive directors and healthcare workers; and Andrea Costella Dawson and Sophie Hagen of W. W. Norton. We also wish to thank Robert Cooke, the CAMH, the actors who brought the material to life, Tom and Reet Mae and Ryan Hannabee of Mae Studios, Bhadra Lokuge, Connie Kim, Lynn Fisher, and Risa Bramon-Garcia.

Series Introduction

Psychotherapy works. Meta-analyses demonstrate that psychotherapy reduces the symptoms and impact of the mental disorders that most commonly interfere with people's lives, including depression, anxiety, and the extraordinary challenges that emerge from concurrent addictions, mental illnesses, and personality disorders. The consensus treatment guidelines that provide clinicians with evidence-based direction for treating depression, anxiety, and other mental disorders recommend psychotherapy, sometimes as a first line of treatment.

At the same time, practicing *effective* psychotherapy is very challenging. For one thing, treatment guidelines recommend specific modalities of psychotherapy for specific disorders, such as Interpersonal Psychotherapy (IPT) for depression, Cognitive Behavioral Therapy (CBT) for depression or anxiety, Motivational Interviewing (MI) for mental health issues and substance abuse disorders, and Dialectical Behavior Therapy (DBT) for borderline personality disorder. Therapists working at the front lines of mental healthcare see *all* of these problems, but acquiring extensive supervision, training, and certification in any one of these modalities is costly and challenging, and being an expert in all types of psychotherapy is virtually impossible. How can a front-line therapist use the core skills of different modalities of psychotherapy effectively to help his or her clients overcome the debilitating effects of mental illness?

Psychotherapy Essentials to Go responds to the challenge that therapists who are not (yet) experts face in acquiring the core skills of psychotherapy. It is designed to be useful for both new therapists and those who are more experienced but want to learn the core techniques of different types of psychotherapy. It also is a refresher course on the techniques that experienced therapists are already familiar with.

This project emerged in response to the needs of mental healthcare workers who were facing extraordinary challenges. Working in community clinics in remote, underserviced areas, these clinicians were unable to provide psychotherapy to their clients because they had minimal psychotherapy training and limited means of acquiring it. Caseloads were often heavy and resources for referring clients to psychotherapists were extremely limited. These clinicians wanted but were unable to use psychotherapeutic techniques to help their clients suffering from depression, anxiety, and concurrent disorders. Needless to say, it was not feasible for these health workers to obtain the training, observation, and close supervision that are required to become experts in specific modalities of psychotherapy. Surely, there was a better alternative than providing no psychotherapy at all!

Drawing on the wealth of expertise of the contributing authors in this series, who are all faculty or staff at teaching hospitals affiliated with the University of Toronto, we created the videos that are at the core of the *Psychotherapy Essentials to Go* materials, as well as all of the accompanying lesson plans in order to meet the needs of clinicians and their clients. The materials worked. We tested the materials that we developed with healthcare workers of several disciplines and levels of experience including the caseworkers in community mental healthcare clinics whose needs initiated the project, medical students, nurses, family medicine and psychiatry residents, and social workers. Their knowledge increased, they used the techniques they had learned, and they reported that they had become more confident and effective clinicians, even with difficult clients. Even seasoned therapists benefited from brushing up on the specific therapy protocols (Ravitz et al., 2013).

The first five books and DVDs of the *Psychotherapy Essentials to Go* series teach the skills of Motivational Interviewing, Cognitive Behavioral Therapy (for anxiety and for depression), Dialectical Behavior Therapy, and Interpersonal Psychotherapy. These materials are not intended to replace full training in these evidence-supported psychotherapies; rather, they introduce and demonstrate techniques that clinicians and students can integrate into their care of people with common mental health problems.

The sixth book and its accompanying DVD address psychotherapy effectiveness across every modality of therapy. Regardless of which type of psychotherapy a therapist provides, doing psychotherapy requires therapists to be flexible and responsive to their clients. Also therapists and clients must form and sustain a strong working relationship: the therapeutic alliance. In every modality of psychotherapy, a good thera-peutic alliance leads to better clinical outcomes. With some clients the challenges encountered in forming and maintaining an alliance provide a window into the interpersonal difficulties that the clients experience in their other important relationships. This final book on psychotherapy effectiveness synthesizes the most important common factors of psycho-therapies and provides a therapist with an approach to understanding and managing challenges to establishing and maintaining a therapeutic alliance.

Learning psychotherapy means *changing how you behave* as a clin-ician—and changing habitual behavior is notoriously difficult. Learning new professional behavior takes time and practice—you need to *experi-ence* a new way of behaving. It isn't enough to read about it or hear about it. Experiential learning is most effective when it includes demonstration, modeling, and practice. For each book in the series, we suggest that you first watch the DVD, then read the accompanying text, and then follow the instructions in the lesson plans to practice and consolidate your learning. Take the quiz before starting this process in order to assess your baseline knowledge, and then take it again after having completed all four of the lessons, in order to assess your progress. Afterward, use the summary card of practice reminders in your daily clinical work.

For those interested in more training, further reading and clinical supervision are recommended. We hope that the techniques presented in these introductory *Psychotherapy Essentials to Go* materials will expand your clinical repertoire and will improve your competence and confi-dence in working with clients with mental health problems.

A couple of notes about language. First, those who provide care and treatment for people with mental health problems, and individuals who receive that care, prefer a wide range of names for those roles, and some have strong feelings about their preferences. For the sake of consistency, throughout this series we refer to the former individuals as "therapists" (occasionally opting for "clinicians" for the sake of some variety of expression) and the latter as "clients." We do this in spite of the fact that some modalities of psychotherapy are explicit about which terms are preferable (for example, IPT manuals refer to the person receiving the therapy as a patient, in keeping with the centrality of the medical model in IPT). We hope these are read to be the inclusive and nonprescriptive choices that are intended. Second, although pronouns in English are gendered, the gender of the therapists and clients we are discussing is usually irrelevant. We have opted for the phrases "he or she" and "his or her" except for a few passages where pronouns were required so frequently that it became too awkward. In those sections we have settled on one gender indiscriminately, with the intention that the "hes" and "shes" will balance out in the end.

Paula Ravitz and Bob Maunder

1 :: Introduction to Cognitive Behavioral Therapy for Anxiety

The fundamentals of contemporary cognitive theory were originally developed by Aaron T. Beck in the latter half of the twentieth century. Beck, who was originally trained as a psychoanalyst, became interested in the unconscious content of the dreams of depressed clients. What he found, however, did not fit the expectations of psychoanalytic theory. Rather than expressing repressed rage, as Freud would have predicted, Beck's subjects dreamed about situations in which they were incompetent or ineffective. Beck's recognition that the Freudian model didn't account for the negative cognitions he was consistently observing (Beck & Hurvich, 1959) led him to develop and describe a new cognitive model of depression. Specifically, he saw that there were strong links among affective states, cognitions, and behaviors, and he recognized that this provided an opening for a new therapeutic paradigm. Beck's Cognitive

Behavioral Treatment (CBT) of depression was rapidly adapted for anxiety and other mental health problems, such that cognitive therapy has become the most empirically validated treatment modality in psychiatry (Beck, Rush, Shaw, & Emery, 1979). There have been numerous studies documenting the efficacy of CBT and supporting its use as a first-line treatment approach, especially for mood and anxiety disorders (Beck, 2005; Clark et al., 1994; Roshanaei-Moghaddam et al., 2011; Stanley, Beck, & Glassco, 1996). As a result, CBT has been included in numerous consensus treatment guidelines for mood and anxiety disorders around the globe (Beck, 2005).

The roots of the behavioral concepts underlying CBT go back considerably further than Beck's work. They originated with Ivan Pavlov's experiments in the 1920s, which demonstrated the phenomena underlying classical conditioning, and their extension to operant conditioning by B. F. Skinner. It was O. Hobart Mowrer who synthesized classical and operant conditioning into a behavioral treatment model in 1947 (reviewed by Hawton, Salkovskis, Kirk, & Clark [1989]). Modern CBT therapists recognize that these two core principles—classical conditioning and operant conditioning—are responsible for generating and maintaining many of the anxious symptoms that arise in response to a variety of stimuli in day-to-day life. In CBT these same principles are adapted to serve recovery instead.

This section provides a user-friendly overview of CBT for the anxiety disorders, written for therapists who already have some experience in the diagnosis and treatment of mental disorders but who are not specifically trained in CBT. It is not our intention to review CBT for anxiety disorders in depth; however, this guide and the accompanying materials provide an excellent point of entry that will enable practitioners to start treatment with this modality. We focus on fundamental skills that are used across the range of anxiety issues, and then we briefly introduce the specifics of their application to the most common anxiety disorders, namely panic disorder (with and without agoraphobia), social anxiety disorder, generalized anxiety disorder (GAD), obsessive-compulsive disorder (OCD), and specific phobias. We have intentionally excluded posttraumatic stress disorder due to the complexity and extra training required to treat clients who have experienced trauma.

TREATMENT ELEMENTS

Current practices incorporate both cognitive and behavioral treatment techniques in the service of symptom reduction and achieving optimal outcomes in anxiety disorders. Several important elements are common across the spectrum of various anxiety disorders.

- Most importantly, people who are anxious tend to overestimate threat, although the nature of the perceived danger may vary with the specific disorder. For example, in panic disorder the focus is on fear of somatic or physical symptoms. In social anxiety disorder, clients overestimate the likelihood of negative judgment and scrutiny by others.
- In addition, sufferers of anxiety disorders underestimate their own ability to cope in the situations that activate these fears.
- Because anxious individuals overestimate threat and underestimate their ability to cope, they often engage in numerous avoidant behav-

iors. These can include overt behaviors, such as leaving or avoiding an anxiety-provoking situation or self-medicating, or more covert strategies, such as distraction or relying on others to help manage their affect.

Behavioral avoidance, while providing initial and short-term relief, serves over time to reinforce clients' underlying pathogenic beliefs by preventing engagement in situations that might provide disconfirmatory evidence. As a result, distorted cognitions are maintained and tend to further generalize over time, leading to broader dysfunction. In the CBT of anxiety, cognitions (overestimating risks and underestimating coping skills) and behaviors (avoidance) are targets for therapeutic intervention with the specific techniques that we describe below and demonstrate in the accompanying videos.

THE CBT THERAPIST STANCE

The CBT therapist adopts a stance that focuses on the "here and now." He or she works collaboratively, engaging with the client to enable the mutual discovery of a more realistic or adaptive perspective. The core techniques used to achieve collaborative, mutual discovery in CBT are Socratic questioning and gathering empirical evidence. Socratic questioning involves asking questions that are designed to better understand the client's difficulties in a nonjudgmental fashion. For example, the CBT therapist would not tell a client who wishes to engage more socially how to do so; instead he would elicit from the client a specific and relevant behavioral task that involves social engagement and would then help identify either potential obstacles the client may encounter or the client's beliefs and fears. This technique is demonstrated in the role-playing in the accompanying video. Empiric evidence gathering refers to collecting information about a client's prior experiences to help disconfirm (or occasionally support!) his anxiety-provoking beliefs. One technique that assists with empiric evidence gathering is the use of the Automatic Thought Record, described on page 7. This process results in clients forming their own more balanced conclusions regarding their beliefs or the value of anxiety-related behaviors.

THE STRUCTURE OF CBT

Because CBT is a short-term intervention, some structure to the overall therapy and the individual sessions is helpful to maintain focus on the most relevant issues. The early phase of therapy includes psychoeducation, orientation to the treatment model, and setting of goals. Psycho-education about the nature of the client's illness and symptoms is a very important early step that helps to normalize her experience. Education should include relevant information about anxiety disorders and the available treatment options, including drug treatment alternatives when these are relevant. "Socialization to the model" is a phrase often used to describe the treatment parameters, framework, and the importance of behavioral tasks in CBT. As with most short-term therapies, clients are also engaged in setting specific, measurable, and achievable goals for the course of treatment. Typical goals for someone with panic disorder/agoraphobia might include being able to venture into previously fearful situations such as walking through crowds or taking public transportation. In the case of social anxiety, a client may want to be able to ask directions of strangers or speak in front of a group of one's peers. A client with GAD may want to use learning techniques to recognize and manage her anxiety-related thoughts and behaviors in the face of stressful events. A client with OCD might try to touch doorknobs, shake hands with people, or leave home without using checking rituals. Specific phobias are usually very straightforward as the aim is to overcome the excessive anxiety provoked by the phobic trigger (i.e., heights, injections, flying, spiders).

Following an agreement on goals, the middle phase of treatment generally focuses on the acquisition of skills and the implementation of more adaptive behaviors. These efforts are consolidated through the use of collaboratively assigned homework to be completed between sessions. Homework is an essential component of CBT, serving to reinforce the mastery of skills and to provide opportunities to challenge long-held dysfunctional beliefs. Homework also serves as an important marker of adherence, motivation, and progress, and it provides a tool to more easily identify real-life obstacles that may interfere with the client's success after termination.

Each individual session generally follows a structured approach. Typical elements would include an update of important events since the last session, a check on core mood and anxiety symptoms, the setting of a collaborative agenda, a review of homework (including problem solving if needed), and the establishment of new homework tasks. Checking in on the therapeutic relationship and the client's sense of alliance with the therapist are particularly important for clients with anxiety disorders.

In preparing for termination, it is desirable to identify with clients their thoughts and feelings related to the end of therapy, and therapists must provide support and techniques that will help clients to move forward. Additionally, one would typically discuss how to recognize and prevent a relapse of symptoms.

CBT TECHNIQUES

The best way to understand CBT techniques and their application is by watching the video and reading the accompanying study guide. In addition, we have picked a few of the most relevant, useful, and accessible techniques to describe here briefly. The interested reader should also refer to the sources within the references list.

The Automatic Thought Record

The thought record is a seven-column tool that helps clients to identify thoughts and feelings in specific situations that trigger anxiety. These thoughts are called "automatic thoughts" because they occur spontaneously in a situation and are usually accepted as being valid without questioning. Although some clients will readily identify automatic thoughts, others need Socratic questioning or the use of the Downward Arrow Technique (shown in the video) in order to recognize them. The thought record goes on to elaborate the evidence that supports or goes against the client's initial anxious thoughts. The sixth column allows for the development of a "balanced thought," reflecting a more accurate view of the situation than the client's initial biased perceptions. The final column asks clients to rate their mood states so as to make the emotional impact of this new balanced way of thinking more concrete.

Interoceptive Exposure

This technique, which involves controlled exposure to body sensations that trigger anxiety, is typically used with clients experiencing panic attacks, whether they occur in the context of panic disorder or another anxiety condition. For many clients, any symptoms reminiscent of a panic attack become major triggers of anxiety. Therefore, interoceptive exposure involves engaging in activities that cause physical symptoms akin to those experienced in a panic attack. This allows clients to learn to habituate to the physical sensations they fear, and it provides an opportunity to challenge dysfunctional beliefs about the dangerousness of these symptoms. For example, hyperventilation is commonly used to intentionally bring on light-headedness, a feeling of shortness of breath, or dizziness. This technique is demonstrated in the accompanying video, and there are a number of other methods listed in the study guide.

Development of Hierarchies and Systematic Desensitization

Given how pervasive avoidant behavior is in anxiety disorders, a hierarchy is often used to collaboratively develop a list of feared situations that will be tackled during therapy. This list is organized according to the intensity of the anxiety triggered and/or the degree of avoidance. Typically, clients are encouraged to begin with easier and less frightening tasks in order to gain mastery. As their confidence increases and anxiety diminishes through practice in sessions and homework, clients gradually move up the hierarchy toward more challenging situations. This behavioral exposure is termed "systematic desensitization." In the video we demonstrate how a panic-related hierarchy is constructed. Sample hierarchy forms are also included in the study guide.

SPECIFIC DISORDERS

Panic Disorder, With or Without Agoraphobia
The core feature of panic disorder is recurrent unexpected panic attacks. Typically clients will overestimate the danger of these symptoms, believing that they are having a heart attack, that they are dying, or that the symptoms themselves are potentially dangerous. They may also develop fears of going "crazy" or of losing control. As a result, clients often avoid situations that could trigger these symptoms, leading to restricted activity, such as ceasing regular exercise, avoiding stairs, or other activities associated with feared symptoms. Additionally, many clients over time develop agoraphobia, which is a fear of going into situations where help may not be readily available or from which it is difficult to exit quickly. This may include fears of crowded places, venturing farther from home than usual, buses or subways, elevators, lineups, movie theaters, and the like.

Cognitive Behavioral Therapy addresses both thoughts and behaviors. From a cognitive perspective, catastrophic thoughts are evaluated for their validity. This is typically done using the thought record. There may also be an opportunity to enhance a client's sense of being able to cope by examining beliefs about her own strength and resilience. Interoceptive exposure is often introduced early in treatment to assist in challenging maladaptive beliefs regarding the dangerousness of panic symptoms. Tackling the client's avoidant behaviors is also essential in restoring health and function. This is generally done through the use of systematic desensitization. An individualized hierarchy is developed, after which clients are encouraged to gradually engage in the listed activities in a sequential fashion from easiest to hardest.

Social Anxiety Disorder

This disorder is characterized by fears of negative evaluation or scrutiny by others, often accompanied by worry of humiliation, in keeping with a belief about a reduced ability to cope. Clients may also believe that they are inherently uninteresting, have nothing to say, or say the wrong thing. They may also focus on fears that anxiety-related symptoms, such as blushing, sweating, or tremors, will be observed and result in further negative evaluation by others. As a result, clients with social anxiety disorder tend to avoid social encounters or situations where they may be the center of attention, such as public speaking, attending parties, dating, or talking to strangers. In severe cases, socially phobic individuals may even avoid eye contact, which may ironically contribute to their behavior seeming odd to others.

In treatment, the dysfunctional cognitions must be identified and addressed through use of the Automatic Thought Record or other techniques. Behavioral techniques are also extremely important in order to challenge avoidant behavior. This is done through use of a hierarchy and exposure as described above. In addition to individualized treatment, group formats may be useful because exposure to social interaction is built into the structure of the treatment. Videotaping to allow clients to observe themselves interacting socially may be extremely helpful, as can participating in organizations such as Toastmasters.

Generalized Anxiety Disorder

There are several cognitive models of GAD but each includes the basic paradigm of overestimation of risk and underestimation of coping skills. Leahy (2005) writes about the worries associated with GAD as being themselves a coping strategy. He argues that the essential fear in GAD is a fear of uncertainty. As a result, these clients worry about things like their health and the future (i.e., things that are inherently uncertain). Leahy suggests that GAD sufferers perpetually worry about these issues as a way of reducing uncertainty. People with GAD will often describe their worries as protective because they serve to reduce uncertainty by playing out various scenarios. However, this is a strategy that is ultimately limited because complete certainty is never possible.

Cognitively, clients' thoughts about the value of their worry can be challenged. Behaviorally, clients may be asked to designate a specific worry time or to record their worries in a log as a way to try and control their anxious thoughts and come to understand them as ultimately unhelpful. Furthermore, these clients generally benefit from gradually being exposed to uncertain situations of increasing magnitudes in order to learn that these situations can be tolerated.

Specific Phobias

Typical phobias tend to fall into four common categories: animals, the natural environment (i.e., storms, heights, or water), blood/injection/

injury, and situational (e.g., public transportation, flying, driving, or being in enclosed places). Individuals typically endure these situations with marked anxiety or avoid them if possible. Phobias can be overcome by facing the things that are feared. This serves to reduce the perception of danger and also to challenge clients' beliefs about their inability to cope. Furthermore, there is a reduction in physical symptomatology as clients become habituated by repeated exposure to triggers. For some extremely anxious clients, exposures may begin with simply hearing the name of the feared situation or viewing a static image of a trigger, then gradually building up to being within the phobic situation itself. These disorders are among the most responsive to treatment of the anxiety disorders and typically resolve over the course of just a few sessions.

Obsessive-Compulsive Disorder
OCD is characterized by its core features: obsessions and compulsions. Obsessions are experienced as intrusive, unwanted, and anxiety-provoking thoughts, images, or impulses that the individual is unable to suppress. Compulsions are repetitive behaviors or mental acts performed in response to obsessions, and they are typically seen as a way to reduce the likelihood of feared events occurring. The most familiar symptom profiles are fears of dirt or contamination obsessions, which usually go along with hand washing and other cleaning rituals, or thoughts of terrible things happening to oneself or loved ones, such as an accident or causing a fire by leaving the stove on, which provoke checking compulsions. However OCD symptoms may vary widely, from needing symmetry or order for things to feel "just right" to repetitive disturbing sexual or sacrilegious thoughts. Associated rituals may include repetitive

actions (i.e., retracing steps or repeatedly closing a door), counting, or thinking a "good" thought to counteract an obsession. Hoarding, or the excessive accumulation of belongings due to difficulty discarding and/or compulsive acquiring, has in the past been viewed as a symptom of OCD, but a growing body of research supports distinguishing this from other forms of OCD. Correspondingly, it is likely to be recognized as a distinct independent condition in the near future.

As with the other anxiety disorders, maladaptive cognitions can be effectively targeted. Key OCD domains include overestimation of risk, excessive perceived responsibility, and the importance and meaning attributed to the obsessions. However, due to the complexity of this condition, behavioral strategies are more straightforward for relatively inexperienced clinicians to effectively implement. In OCD the focus is on exposure to the obsessional triggers, partnered with "exposure and response prevention" (ERP), in which the client is encouraged to abstain from the attendant rituals. Avoidance must also be identified and challenged in sessions. Thus, for an individual who fears germs, an initial goal might be to touch doorknobs (exposure) without hand washing (response prevention). This would be followed by encouragement to then touch "clean" things (such as one's face, watch, wallet, cellphone, etc.) to target avoidance behaviors. Other safety behaviors that may serve to sustain symptoms (such as seeking reassurance or mental reviewing) should also be identified and challenged in subsequent sessions. ERP progresses hierarchically but may require more practice between sessions (ideally daily) and a longer course of treatment to get optimum improvement.

CONCLUSION

Cognitive Behavioral Therapy is an evidence-based approach to several common psychiatric conditions, including anxiety disorders. It provides a unique approach and structure to the treatment of these disorders. While there have been criticisms leveled against CBT as being too dogmatic or even robotic, the modern CBT therapist is a skilled and sophisticated thinker. In addition to an important understanding of the cognitive and behavioral factors that lead to the generation and maintenance of these disorders, a good CBT therapist must know how to collaboratively incorporate new skills and experiments into the therapy. Furthermore, careful attention to the therapeutic relationship and the thoughts and feelings generated by it in both parties of the dyad is essential to good outcomes. So we encourage you to read, watch videos, and access other resources while you immerse yourself in the world of CBT, but be sure to leave some space for the other person who is in the room with you.

2 :: Learning Objectives

Anxiety disorders are the most common psychiatric disorders. They cause a great deal of suffering and can interfere enormously with people's lives, as you saw in the case of "Kathy" in the accompanying video. Fortunately, there are very effective techniques that you can learn in order to help treat clients with anxiety disorders.

In this module, we will teach you very specific cognitive and behavioral techniques that will reduce anxiety and improve your clients' function. By the end of this module we hope that you'll be able to understand the cognitive model for anxiety disorders in general and panic disorder in particular. In addition, we'll teach you specific interview techniques that will help you identify the thoughts associated with anxiety. Finally, you will learn how to apply basic behavioral and cognitive techniques to help clients with anxiety: for example, using cognitive restructuring, using the

Automatic Thought Record, using interoceptive exposure, and using a fear hierarchy and graded exposure.

At the end of this book, we hope that you will be able to achieve these goals:

1. Understand the cognitive model for anxiety disorders in general and panic disorder in particular.
2. Utilize focused interviewing techniques to identify key anxious thoughts.
3. Apply cognitive and behavioral techniques for anxiety.
4. Perform cognitive restructuring using an Automatic Thought Record.
5. Practice interoceptive exposure.
6. Develop a fear hierarchy and plan graded exposure.

Mark Fefergrad and Peggy Richter

3 :: Fundamentals of CBT for Anxiety

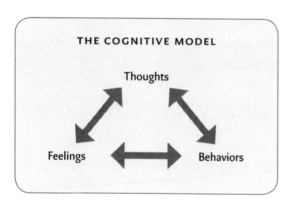

THE COGNITIVE MODEL

Thoughts

Feelings ⟷ Behaviors

THE COGNITIVE MODEL

The basic cognitive model is very simple. Essentially it says that every moment in your life can be broken down into three basic components:

- How you are feeling emotionally—such as happy, sad, angry, or anxious;
- What you are thinking: what thoughts are going through your head; and
- Your behavior and what you're doing.

The idea is that all of these components interact with one another. In other words, how you think about something affects how you feel about it. How you feel about someone affects how you behave toward them, and so on. The issue for clients with anxiety is that none of us control our emotions directly. However, because all of these things interact with one another, we can learn to change how we feel by changing how we think and how we behave. So by helping clients learn to think and behave differently, you can actually help people to feel better, which is the ultimate goal of Cognitive Behavioral Therapy.

FOCUSING ON AVOIDANCE

Typically, people who have anxiety disorders tend to overestimate possible dangers and tend to underestimate their own ability to cope. As you can imagine, if someone thinks that something is very dangerous and that he can't handle it, it is natural for him to try to avoid that frightening thing. The first goal of CBT is not necessarily to reduce the number of panic attacks for someone who experiences anxiety in the form of panic; rather, you need to help the client to think a little differently about the panic attacks, so that he or she no longer feels the need to avoid the thing that provokes anxiety. Although it isn't the primary goal, symptom reduction often follows.

KEY POINTS OF CBT

1. Feelings are linked to thoughts and behaviors.
2. Just because you think something doesn't necessarily mean that it is true.
3. CBT helps clients think realistically in a balanced way.
4. Thoughts can be examined cognitively or tested behaviorally.
5. New behaviors can serve to alter thoughts or gather facts.
6. How you think about events is more important than the events themselves.

KEY POINTS OF CBT

There are a few key points related to CBT.

First, according to the cognitive model, feelings are linked to thoughts and behaviors.

Second, just because you think something doesn't necessarily mean that it's true. The philosophical stance we take in CBT is that we want to be very skeptical of our thoughts. For example, you might plan to attend a gathering but think that "it is not going to be fun at all." You go to the gathering in spite of your expectations and find that it turns out to be much more enjoyable than expected. This is a familiar example of how our thoughts are not totally accurate. In CBT, we ask clients to experiment with thoughts like these to test their validity.

Third, a CBT therapist does not aim to have clients think positively about everything. That's likely unrealistic. There are some events in life that are simply not positive. However, CBT does help you to think about things realistically in a balanced way. According to the CBT model, if you're able to do that, your emotions will also be balanced and correspond to the situation in which you find yourself.

Next, thoughts can be examined in a variety of ways. The Automatic Thought Record is a CBT tool for examining thoughts. In addition, we can also test thoughts behaviorally.

Sometimes we ask a client to enact a new behavior in the service of potentially verifying or falsifying some of his or her thoughts, or perhaps just gathering new evidence or new pieces of information.

Lastly, and perhaps most important, it's not the event that is most important in CBT: It's how you think about it. If we focus on panic attacks, as Kathy describes, it's not the panic attack that's most important; it's how she thinks about it. If she thinks, "This panic attack is going to kill me; I can't survive it, so this means that I'm going to die; I'm going to have a heart attack," her thoughts cause serious problems. However, if she thinks, "This is something I can cope with; it's uncomfortable but manageable," she has a very different kind of experience, one that leads to a much more happy and functional life.

Generally speaking, you'll be seeing clients no more than once a week in order to consolidate some of the skills that CBT tries to build. In addition, clients will need to practice on their own outside of sessions. Clients who come to you asking for a medication or a quick fix, who are not really willing to look at the thoughts behind their anxiety, or who are unwilling to put themselves in an anxiety-provoking situation with proper support and guidance are unlikely to benefit from this kind of therapy.

CBT ESSENTIAL QUESTIONS

What are the. . .
- client's most important problems to work on now?
- cognitions or automatic thoughts that interfere with the client's life and problem solving?
- techniques that can help the client to see the problem in a more adaptive way in order to improve functioning?

CBT ESSENTIAL QUESTIONS

There are a few essential questions, you want to ask yourself whenever you're treating someone using CBT techniques. First, what is the client's most important problem to work on right now? CBT really aims to treat the things that are most important and most affecting the client.

Second, what cognitions or automatic thoughts are interfering with this client's way of life or problem solving?

Finally, you always want to be strategic in terms of thinking about what techniques you can apply to help a client view himself or view the world in ways that are more functional and more adaptive.

SOCRATIC QUESTIONING AND GUIDED DISCOVERY

SOCRATIC QUESTIONING AND GUIDED DISCOVERY

"In the best cognitive therapy there are no answers, only good questions that guide the discovery of a million different individual answers."

- What would happen if this were true?
- How likely do you think this is?
- What would you say to a friend in the same situation?

A CBT therapist likes to use Socratic questioning. This means that rather than giving clients the answers to questions, we want to ask those questions that will allow clients to come to their own conclusions.

There's a great quote that says, "In the best cognitive therapy there are no answers, only good questions that guide the discovery of a million different individual answers." So, for example, for a client with panic disorder like Kathy, rather than just telling her that "the panic attacks are not dangerous, you won't die from them, you can survive them," you want to ask her the questions and get her to engage in the kinds of behaviors that will allow her to discover solutions for herself.

Examples of Socratic questioning include the following:

- What would happen if this were true?
- How likely do you think this is?
- What would you say to a friend who was in the same situation?

FEAR VERSUS ANXIETY

> **FEAR VERSUS ANXIETY**
>
> Fear is the normal and healthy response to a threat
>   and it enhances survival.
>
> Anxiety is inappropriate or excessive fear.

One of the important issues that needs to be addressed in educating clients about the cognitive model is that fear is normal and healthy. We all need to experience fear in situations that demand it. For example, anyone who realizes that he or she is about to be involved in a traffic accident is likely to experience a healthy fear response. If we are in a situation like that, we expect our heart rates to go up, to feel a little short of breath, and to feel on edge and very pumped up. Fear in circumstances like that is a healthy survival response. The issue with anxiety disorders is that people have this fear response in situations where there may be no threat or where the response is exaggerated or unnecessary.

ANXIETY VERSUS PANIC

ANXIETY VERSUS PANIC

Chronic Anxiety—fluctuates over hours, days
Panic Attack—a discrete period of intense fear, discomfort, and anxiety with:
- Sudden onset
- A duration of 15 to 60 minutes
- Physical symptoms including increased heart rate; shortness of breath; feeling faint, sweaty, dizzy, shaky; stomach distress
- Fears of losing control, dying, or "going crazy"

Once clients understand that anxiety is occurring in situations where there is no real threat, the next step is to help them to distinguish normal transient anxiety from chronic problematic anxiety. We all know what anxiety is. We all feel it in varying circumstances from time to time. People with anxiety disorders experience this tension and worry more chronically: their anxious feelings can linger over hours or days and can come in waves that rise and recede slowly.

Panic, by contrast, comes in sharp, sudden attacks or surges in which people experience very intense anxiety. Characteristically, panic involves the sudden onset of a really dramatic upswing in anxiety associated with a host of physical symptoms that usually do not last very long. Typically, panic attacks are over within 15 minutes to an hour, although people may take many hours after that to actually feel like themselves again.

MEDICAL CONDITIONS

MEDICAL CONDITIONS, MEDICATIONS, AND DRUGS CAN BRING ON SYMPTOMS OF ANXIETY

Screen for:
- Heart conditions, asthma, low blood sugar, thyroid problems
- Medications or foods (caffeine)
- Drugs of abuse and withdrawal symptoms
- Alcohol/marijuana commonly used by clients to decrease anxiety can precipitate panic/anxiety in their withdrawal phase

A number of medical conditions can masquerade as anxiety disorders, and a number of prescription and street drugs that individuals may take can also create presentations that look like anxiety disorders.

In order to be sure that what looks like an anxiety disorder is actually anxiety, it is important to be aware of medical conditions that can simulate anxiety symptoms: for example, cardiovascular illness, to consider whether the client may be having a heart attack, asthma, low blood sugar episodes, or thyroid abnormalities.

Many prescription medications can bring on more rapid heart rates or other symptoms that resemble anxiety. Street drugs can also have that effect, either during periods of intoxication or withdrawal. Caffeine and other stimulants are very common culprits with effects that mimic anxiety.

These are all things that should be screened when you are first assessing clients with apparent anxiety disorders. Therapists who are not physicians should ensure that clients have had a medical assessment before they are treated for anxiety disorders.

4 :: Beginning CBT for Anxiety

Although CBT works most effectively through Socratic questioning and new experiences that change excessively frightening thoughts, it is still important in the beginning to provide some basic information, which includes talking to clients about general lifestyle issues. Many things may make anxiety better or worse. Getting a good night's sleep can make a big difference, as can minimizing the use of sedatives and hypnotics, getting regular exercise, and practicing relaxation techniques.

Right from the start we give clients the message that panic attacks are not life-threatening. Of course, the CBT therapist also instills hope with the explicit message that CBT is likely to be very helpful in reducing distress.

COGNITIVE MODEL OF PANIC DISORDER

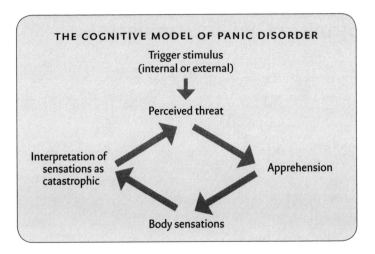

People with anxiety tend to overestimate the dangerousness of a situation, overestimate the dangerousness of their symptoms and their thoughts, and, as we also heard before, underestimate their ability to cope with these situations (Clark, 1986).

Using this as a model, we can imagine that a person who is in a situation where something triggers his anxiety symptoms may develop physical symptoms, like we heard about from Kathy: feelings of dizziness or faintness, the heart beating too rapidly, or shortness of breath. However, those symptoms alone won't be enough, necessarily, to cause panic. In addition, expectations based on previous experiences, beliefs, or appraisals of the dangerousness of the situation or physical symptoms amplify the person's difficulty. As apprehension grows, it sets off a vicious cycle, causing even more anxiety because of the fearful thoughts it brings.

WHAT DO YOU FEAR WILL HAPPEN?

In CBT, we ask clients what they really fear. In panic disorder it's often the thought that they will have a panic attack. Looking a little deeper, you find a fear of fainting and perhaps being embarrassed or a more emotion-laden thought that they will die from their anxiety.

A client with social phobia usually fears humiliating or embarrassing herself. How will she seem in front of others? Will people think that she looks odd or sounds silly?

With generalized anxiety disorder, fears are usually focused on very realistic worries that everyone experiences from time to time. The problem isn't with the content of the worries; it is their persistence and the degree to which they dominate people's thoughts.

WHAT DO YOU FEAR WILL HAPPEN?

Panic Disorder
I will have a panic attack.
I will be unable to escape or function.
I will die from my anxiety.

Social Phobia
I will embarrass myself.
I will be humiliated.
I will fail under scrutiny.

Generalized Anxiety Disorder
Recurrent and intrusive worries that something
    realistically bad could happen to me or my family
    such as:
        Death/illness
        Financial problems

Obsessive Compulsive Disorder (OCD)
Intrusive thoughts that something very bad
    will happen and it will be my fault:
The door is left unlocked . . . and will result
    in a break-in.
The stove is left on . . . and will start a fire.
If I touch anything dirty, . . . I'll get sick or
    make others sick.
I'll think bad thoughts . . . and they will come true.
If I don't [get up from a chair, close a door,
    step on a crack] just right, . . . something
    bad will happen.

With obsessive-compulsive disorder (OCD), the fear often focuses on very bad things happening. A person may worry about leaving the door unlocked and therefore being responsible for a break-in; she may worry that leaving the stove on will lead to a fire; he may believe that touching something dirty will make him sick or, even worse, that he could make others ill. Sometimes people with OCD have intrusive, disturbing thoughts. These may be thoughts that all of us have from time to time (that something terrible is going to happen), except that with OCD an additional fear arises: that the thinking itself is dangerous, that having the thoughts makes them more likely to come true, or that this reflects badly on the thinker.

5 :: Cognitive Techniques

INTERVIEW TECHNIQUES AND
THE AUTOMATIC THOUGHT RECORD

If a client thinks, "This is something I can handle," rather than, "If I have a panic attack I'll die," he is much less likely to experience anxiety. One of the mechanisms that CBT therapists use to achieve this cognitive restructuring is called the Automatic Thought Record.

There are actually many different versions of the Automatic Thought Record. The version we recommend is reprinted with permission from its creator, Dr. Christine Padesky, the co-author with Dennis Greenberger of the very well-known CBT self-help book *Mind Over Mood* (Greenberger & Padesky, 1995).

Column #1 is labeled "Situation." The situation has to be a very specific moment in time when the client noticed some change in emotion. It should not be something like "the time I was arguing with my wife" because arguments can take place over quite a long time. Rather, we want the client to identify a single moment when his emotions started to change. This is important for two reasons. First, the thoughts in that moment are going to be the thoughts that we most want to alter. Second, referring to a very specific situation helps clients get better in touch with the emotions and thoughts that they were experiencing.

Column #2 is "Moods." Here's where the client lists any emotions that he was feeling in the situation he described in Column #1. A mood, generally speaking, can be a single word—happy, sad, angry, or anxious. The client should also rate the intensity of those moods in this column from 0 to 100 percent, where 0 is not experiencing that emotion at all and 100 is the most intensely he has ever experienced that emotion.

Column #3 captures the automatic thoughts. These are the thoughts that spontaneously come unbidden to the client's mind. Again, remember, the client must focus on only that moment when he experienced a specific change in emotion. CBT assumes that any thoughts that were going on at that precise period are related to the emotional state. Once all of the automatic thoughts have been generated, the client must identify one of those thoughts as the "hot thought." The hot thought is affectively hot. It is the thought that is most driving the emotion that was described in Column #2. All the subsequent columns will work exclusively with the hot thought because that's the thought where the client really wants to direct attention and energy.

AUTOMATIC THOUGHT RECORD

Situation	Moods	Automatic Thought	Evidence that Supports the Hot Thought	Evidence that Doesn't Support the Hot Thought	Alternative Balanced Thought	Rate Mood
Tuesday: Walk into store and see how many people are there @9:30 or 10 am	Panic 100% Scared 80% Worried 60% Embarrassed 45%	–I'm in trouble –It's going to happen –I was going to die (hot thought) –Surrounded by strangers	Chest was tight Hands and arms tingled Couldn't catch breath Hot and sweaty From med professional: signs of a potential heart attack	Emergency room checked heart & lungs & everything worked fine Can get hot & sweaty, or tingly arms and fingers when in other situations	Although I thought I was going to die because my chest got tight & I knew that was evidence that I was going to have a heart attack, I kept breathing & I didn't turn blue & the doctors told me that my heart & lungs were fine	50%

© Center for Cognitive Therapy, www.padesky.com; 7-Column Thought Record used with permission; © 1983 Christine A. Padesky, PhD.

Columns #4 and #5 both speak to evidence. Column #4 is evidence that supports the hot thought, whereas Column #5 lists evidence that does not support the hot thought, sometimes known as the contra evidence. This is an opportunity for the client to generate all the objective pieces of facts that either support or do not support the hot thought. This allows him to think in a more objective way. The client should provide evidence that is objectively provable, like in a court of law.

In Column #6 you and your client will rewrite the hot thought in a fashion that is totally based on the evidence that he has generated. This alternative evidence-based thought stands in opposition to the automatic thought that came from the client's biases based on his own ways of thinking and prior experiences. Rather, the thought in Column #6 takes into account all the available evidence that is objectively provable.

Finally, Column #7 is the payoff. The CBT therapist asks the client to re-rate the intensity of the moods that are listed in Column #2. If all has gone well, there should be a decrease in some of the negative emotions, as a result of a more balanced way of thinking.

QUESTIONS TO IDENTIFY AUTOMATIC THOUGHTS

- What was going through your mind just then?
- What do you think you were thinking about?
- What did the situation mean to you (or mean about you)?
- Do you think you could have been thinking _____?

It's important to know what kinds of questions you can ask a client in order to generate the automatic thoughts that will be recorded in Column #3. One question you might ask is "What was going through your mind just then?" Another possibility is "What do you think you were thinking about?" You might also ask, "What did the situation mean to you (or mean about you)?"

Finally, as a last resort, because we're trying to use Socratic questioning and guided discovery, you might ask, "Do you think you could have been thinking _____?" We want to leave this option as a last resort because it is more effective for clients to come up with their own answers.

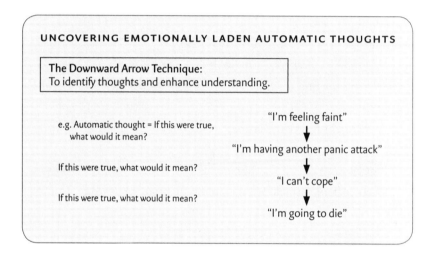

UNCOVERING EMOTIONALLY LADEN AUTOMATIC THOUGHTS

Another important cognitive technique is the Downward Arrow Technique. This is a strategy that helps the client to identify thoughts that are a little bit hotter and that are more likely to be generating the emotion. Sometimes a client will come up with thoughts for Column #3 that are not quite hot enough and we can help her by asking a few gentle questions to get closer to the thoughts that are most driving the emotion. This is a very simple technique where you might ask something like "What does that mean?" or "What does that say about you?"

For example, a client with panic disorder might have the thought "I'm feeling faint." Well, that's an important thought but it is probably not the hot thought. Given that this client has an anxiety disorder, it is likely that the trigger for the feeling is something more frightening.

So you might ask, "If it were true that you were feeling faint, what would that mean?" or "What would that say?"

And the client might say, "Oh no, it's happening again."

And so you might ask, "If it's true that it's happening again, what does that say?"

And she might respond, "It means that I'm having another panic attack."

You might push a little further and ask, "If it were true that you were having another panic attack, what would that say or what would that mean?"

And your client might answer, "Well, that means that I can't cope."

Going even one step further, you might ask, "If it were true that you couldn't cope, what do you think would happen or what does that mean?"

To which the client may answer, "That means I'm going to die."

You can see that this final thought is much more emotionally laden than some of those earlier thoughts. Although the Automatic Thought Record can be used for any thought, we ideally want to use it to tackle the hottest thoughts, and that's the reason we use the Downward Arrow Technique to get to those thoughts that are most associated with the emotion. Working on those thoughts is going to be the most efficient way of helping the client to change an emotional state.

MONITORING TREATMENT SYMPTOMS

Encourage clients to use diaries and self-ratings of symptoms:

Anxiety, cognitions, rituals, homework

- Duration
- Anxiety severity (0–100%)
- Physical symptoms
- When and where (time and place)
- Automatic thoughts

MONITORING TREATMENT SYMPTOMS

There are some very useful tools that help clinicians monitor the effectiveness of treatment, and, even more importantly, they can help the clients see for themselves how things are changing over time. Keeping a diary is one of the most important of these tools. A diary can be very idiosyncratic; there is no one ingredient that must absolutely be included. It is often useful, however, to get clients to begin to document events where they have experienced anxiety, the thoughts that went with it, and perhaps the situations that triggered it. If they have rituals that go with the anxiety, such as washing their hands or checking things, these can be written down as well. Keeping careful track of their homework helps. It is important for clients to keep in mind things like the duration of the symptoms and to get comfortable with rating the intensity of moods.

We want individuals to experience the positive reinforcement that comes with seeing improvement in these things that have been problems.

Nothing helps people feel more motivated to continue with CBT like seeing for themselves that they've actually begun to make a little difference. It's also a really great tool for clinicians to help the clients problem solve if things aren't going quite as we expected they would.

6 :: Behavioral Techniques

AVOIDANCE—THE "ENEMY" OF CBT

- When clients believe that a situation is dangerous or that they cannot cope with it, avoidance is a predictable behavior.
- Avoidance works to reduce anxiety and is highly reinforced—"I feel better; therefore, I must have done the right thing."
- HOWEVER, when clients avoid, they deprive themselves of an opportunity to learn that they can cope with the feared situation.

AVOIDANCE

When beginning to plan a course of CBT with the client, it's important to make him aware of the role of avoidance in maintaining and sustaining difficulties. People avoid situations that they feel are dangerous when they believe they can't cope. In anxiety disorders this combination occurs frequently. Your client needs your help to begin to identify his avoidance. As he pays attention to what he is avoiding, he also needs to understand that avoidance is preventing him from developing feelings of confidence in his ability to deal with these situations. He is robbing himself of opportunities to challenge some of the dysfunctional beliefs he holds about his inability to deal with the frightening situation or about the situation's dangerousness. Avoidance maintains a vicious cycle of increasing anxiety.

Avoidance comes in many forms. It may be obvious, such as when a person leaves a situation that triggers anxiety or chooses not to go there in the first place. Avoidance can also be more subtle.

> **TYPES OF AVOIDANCE**
>
> - Leaving or not going into situations
> - Cognitive avoidance (not thinking about things)
> - Alcohol
> - Drugs (illicit and short-acting anxiolytics)
> - Distraction
> - "Coping" strategies, like never being alone

Using substances before going into an anxiety-provoking situation is a way of avoiding intense anxiety. The substance may allow a person to feel ready for the situation, but it may also prevent her from thinking all the automatic thoughts that would usually occur.

Clients may distract themselves by thinking of other things and thereby not really let themselves think about the triggers of their anxiety.

They may use other kinds of coping strategies, like keeping a trusted significant other with them or keeping something else nearby to lean on if they worry about being faint. This helps to reduce anxiety in the short term but prevents the client from challenging her assumptions about the situation's dangers and her ability to cope with it on her own.

People can come up with all kinds of strategies to avoid anxiety. It can become complex, sometimes, to help them begin to identify all of these issues and then begin to remove them, one by one.

MOVING FROM THE COGNITIVE TO THE BEHAVIORAL

In addition to cognitive techniques, the CBT therapist works with behavior to overcome avoidance and to challenge automatic thoughts.

Interoceptive exposure is a core behavioral technique in which clients do exercises that help to bring on some of the symptoms of their anxiety attacks or to amplify anxiety. We combine interoceptive exposure with box breathing, a very effective, easy-to-use relaxation technique that can be done anywhere at any time.

Finally, we guide clients in actual exposure exercises, which are the bread and butter of behavior therapy, where clients really get to begin practicing everything they've learned.

> **MOVING FROM THE COGNITIVE TO THE BEHAVIORAL**
>
> **Identify:**
> Avoidance
>
> **Teach:**
> Interoceptive Exposure
> Box Breathing
> External Exposure

Various techniques can help bring on some of the somatic or physical symptoms people experience when they panic.

Running in place for a minute may be used to bring on a rapid heart rate or shortness of breath.

Spinning in a chair is a great exercise for people who associate feelings of dizziness or light-headedness with their panic attacks, and it is a great way for them to begin to realize that in fact this is not so terrifying after all.

Hyperventilating will bring on a variety of symptoms beginning with light-headedness but also faintness, blurred vision, tingling, and other uncomfortable symptoms.

Another exercise that can work well for a client who fears feeling short of breath is breathing through a straw with her nose plugged, which will really bring on those feelings and help her to develop confidence in her ability to cope.

INTEROCEPTIVE EXPOSURE

Learning to become less frightened by internal symptoms

Technique

- Run in place for 1 min.
- Spin in chair for 1 min.
- Hyperventilate for 1 min.
- Breathe through a straw for 2 mins. with nose plugged

Associated Symptoms

- Fast heart rate
- Dizziness
- Light-headedness, numbness, blurred vision
- Shortness of breath

Box breathing helps individuals learn to become conscious of their breathing patterns and gives them a very deliberate method to slow their breathing down. It is extremely common for a person who is feeling anxious to breathe too rapidly. So with box breathing we encourage people to do the opposite and we focus simply on generating a relaxed, slow rhythm of breathing, which has the effect of reducing anxiety.

Finally, the CBT therapist works with clients to tackle the situations that trigger their anxiety in the real world. This is called exposure, and the core technique in successful exposure is the use of a hierarchy.

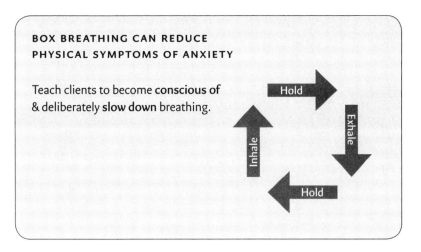

BOX BREATHING CAN REDUCE PHYSICAL SYMPTOMS OF ANXIETY

Teach clients to become **conscious of** & deliberately **slow down** breathing.

The hierarchy lists anxiety-provoking situations that are very specific, very practical, and very detailed so that both the therapist and client know exactly what they need to do. Tasks on the hierarchy need to be practical; they have to be able to fit into a client's daily life so that clients can practice exposing themselves to these triggers on a very regular basis.

Rapid, shallow breathing associated with anxiety

Depth of Inhalation and Exhalation

Time

Slower, deeper breathing during box breathing

Depth of Inhalation and Exhalation

Time

A common beginner's error is to not practice long enough. It is extremely important that clients understand that they need to stay in their exposure situations until the anxiety habituates, meaning that it begins to abate and improve. How long that takes varies from individual to individual, but a good rule of thumb is an hour.

**EXPOSURE USING A FEAR HIERARCHY
(FOR USE WITH ALL ANXIETY DISORDERS)**

- List **specific** anxiety-producing activities and rate them in an ascending order of difficulty.
- Plan practical exposure tasks, starting with the easiest in the ascending order of difficulty.
  - Practice at least three times per week, staying in the activity until anxiety subsides (~ 1 hour).
  - The more often and the longer the exposure, the better!
- Rate anxiety and avoidance before and after exposure (0-100%).
- Anticipate and discuss obstacles.

In working with panic clients, we usually like to emphasize that practice should take place at least three times a week. For those with some of the more difficult-to-treat anxiety disorders like OCD, homework should be done five times a week or, ideally, daily.

7 :: Concluding Remarks

> **THERAPEUTIC REMINDERS: CBT FOR ANXIETY**
>
> Use both cognitive and behavioral techniques:
> 1. <u>Psychoeducation</u>
> 2. <u>Cognitive restructuring</u>: Use the Automatic Thought Record to minimize the sense of danger and increase the sense of self-efficacy
> 3. <u>Interoceptive exposure</u> can help clients to be less afraid of symptoms.
> 4. Graded behavioral exposure by using a <u>fear hierarchy</u> helps clients to disconfirm their fears and confirm their capacity to cope.

Here are some of the most important take-home points from this book and DVD on CBT for anxiety.

- First, remember that in the cognitive model thoughts, feelings, and behaviors are all linked with each other. For anxiety we really want to help the client to understand exactly how he overestimates the threat and the thoughts associated with that threat, and the client must realize that he underestimates his own ability to cope.
- A CBT therapist uses a combination of both cognitive and behavioral techniques to help clients cope with their anxiety disorders.

- Psychoeducation is a very important component of treating anxiety because people need to understand that anxiety, while uncomfortable, is not dangerous.
- Cognitive restructuring by using the Automatic Thought Record is a specific technique that can allow clients to change their thoughts within a moment; specifically, a client can address the thoughts that are most associated with intense feelings of anxiety or panic.
- Interoceptive exposure helps clients learn experientially that some of the physical symptoms they feel in their bodies can be related to normal physiological mechanisms. This can be combined with practicing box breathing to help alleviate anxious feelings.
- Finally, graded behavioral exposure using a fear hierarchy can help provide clients with a systematic way of approaching feared situations so that they can gradually expand the sphere of influence over which they can act.

These are powerful techniques that help clients to improve rapidly. Try them out for yourself and see how they work.

Lesson Plans

(See Appendix C for answers.)

LESSON PLAN #1

The Use of Cognitive Techniques in the Treatment of Anxiety Disorders
Watch Role Play #1 in the video.

A. Discussion

1. List two reasons the information in Column #1 should be as specific as possible.
2. Is suicidality an emotion or a thought?
3. Why is this an important distinction?
4. What is the "hot thought"?
5. Setting aside any other CBT techniques, how do you imagine that just being aware of your thoughts and emotions might be helpful or challenging?

6. Where do automatic thoughts come from?

7. What is the difference between thoughts and evidence?

8. Why do we collect "evidence for" in Column #4?

9. How do you think underlying core beliefs or schemas are generated?

B. **Experiential Tasks**

1. Set an alarm to go off at 4 minutes into the video. At that moment, pay attention to and write down your feelings and thoughts. Be thorough. What do you notice? Is there a connection between the thoughts and emotions? What might help you practice this skill of being more aware of thoughts and feelings?

2. Compile an Automatic Thought Record. You can imagine that you are with a client, or ideally you can work with a colleague or friend. Carefully and slowly complete the first three columns. You may draw from an actual client's story, or you can discuss common work stressors such as not enough work-life balance, being behind on paperwork, or feeling unhelpful or unskilled as a medical practitioner. Make sure you identify and circle the "hot thought." After 10 minutes, if you are working in pairs, swap roles and, once each partner has taken a turn, compare and review experiences.

C. **Homework**

Complete an Automatic Thought Record on at least three different occasions when you notice a change in emotion. Try to complete the thought records as close in time to the emotional shift as you can. Pay attention to any patterns that may emerge between the three thought records.

LESSON PLAN #2
Relaxation Exercises and Interoceptive Exposure
Watch Role Play #2 on relaxation techniques and interoceptive exposure.

Review Homework from Lesson Plan #1

A. Discussion
    1. How does box breathing work?
    2. List two other relaxation techniques.
    3. List three ways in which you can generate interoceptive exposure.
    4. What are the two main "rules" of all exposure?
    5. What if a client develops a full-blown panic attack during an exposure?
    6. Should you administer an anxiolytic medication like a benzodiazepine during an exposure if the client appears anxious?
    7. How might alcohol affect an interoceptive exposure?
    8. Why do clients become distressed when they experience physical sensations in their bodies?
    9. What are some key points to emphasize at the end of the exposure?

B. **Experiential Tasks**
1.   Try doing box breathing for 2 full minutes while sitting calmly at rest. Pay attention to your thoughts and what you notice in your body.
2.   Try running up and down three flights of stairs (or whatever will constitute reasonable exertion given your location and fitness level) and then repeat the box breathing exercise. Pay attention to your thoughts and physical sensations.

C. **Homework**
Try exerting yourself physically on a daily basis. Use box breathing, progressive muscle relaxation, and positive mental imagery to see how well they work for you and where you run into difficulty.

LESSON PLAN #3
Developing and Using an Exposure Hierarchy
Watch Role Play #3 on developing a hierarchy.

Review Homework from Lesson Plan #2

A. **Discussion**
1.   What are the ratings associated with the hierarchy?
2.   Why do we want a steady increase in difficulty over the course of the hierarchy?
3.   What are variables that can be modified in a hierarchy?
4.   What is the role of prediction in a hierarchy?

5. Why don't we start at the top of the hierarchy?
6. What is a SUDS score?
7. How long should a client spend on an individual exposure session?
8. How do you know when to move to the next exposure task?
9. What is the role of thought records in hierarchies/exposures?
10. Can a client "fail" a hierarchy?

B. Experiential Tasks

1. Imagine that you are with a client, or work with a colleague or friend. Write down what you would do to try to convince a client to engage in an exposure task. If you are working in pairs, try to convince your partner to engage in an exposure task. Use psychoeducation, reassurance, logic, and thought records if necessary. Try to understand what motivates your partner (or imaginary client) and use that as leverage.
2. Pick a simple phobia that you or someone you know suffers from (heights, spiders, dentists, needles, blood, flying, snakes, etc.) Try to design a hierarchy that would help you to conquer that fear.

C. Homework

Using the hierarchy you developed, try an exposure task. First, make a prediction about the outcome and the intensity of your anxiety. Then expose yourself to the feared stimulus until your anxiety level decreases by at least 50% from the peak. Graph your anxiety every 5 minutes. Repeat this exercise at least three times over the course of the week. What did you notice?

LESSON PLAN #4
Consolidation and Clinical Applications

Review Homework from Lesson Plan #3

A. Discussion

Case #1: A Case of Panic Disorder With Agoraphobia

Mrs. Chloe Avigrad is a 50-year-old woman who lives in a house with her husband, Andrew. They have been married for the last 23 years. They have two daughters, ages 17 and 20. Chloe has been working in advertising, and although she has been highly successful, she has found it increasingly stressful. Things became much worse several months ago when her firm hired a new manager. This new manager does not seem to respect Chloe's expertise. Furthermore, the manager often criticizes Chloe's work in public office spaces, leaving Chloe feeling humiliated. Lately Chloe has noticed that she now feels anxious and occasionally panicky whenever she needs to talk to co-workers in open spaces at work, even if her manager is not around.

Over the last few weeks, Chloe has developed symptoms consistent with panic disorder. Several times a day, she will have episodes characterized by shortness of breath, heart palpitations, sweating, tremors, tingling, and a sense of losing control. These episodes last approximately 10 minutes each. Chloe is so worried about being admonished further by her boss that at the first sign of these symptoms, she quickly runs to the bathroom stall for privacy. In addition, she has noticed that while she feels great on the weekends, Sunday night is consistently a difficult time. She describes stomach upset as well as difficulty falling asleep on Sunday evening.

More recently, Chloe has kept an eye out for her boss while working in the office. If she has the sense that her boss may come over to her work space, she will pretend to be busy on the phone with a client or sometimes even leave the office altogether.

Case #1

1. What do you imagine are some of Chloe's thoughts with respect to her physical symptoms?
2. How would you counsel Chloe with respect to her work situation?
3. What are some of the advantages and disadvantages of providing Chloe with an as-needed anxiolytic agent like a benzodiazepine?
4. Can you think of things Chloe might be able to do to enhance her sense of being able to cope with her critical boss?
5. How might you use the fact that Chloe is in advertising to your therapeutic advantage?

Case #2: A Case of Social Anxiety

Ms. Elsie Roseman is a 24-year-old single woman. Her parents both have doctorates in chemistry and rarely socialize with other people. Elsie has always felt like she doesn't measure up to her parents intellectually. They seem to value publications and discoveries in the world of academia whereas Elsie is far more interested in the arts. Although Elsie graduated from a well-regarded university, she has struggled since then, generally working at solitary and somewhat uninteresting office jobs in isolation. She has also gained 35 pounds over the last 2 years. Most of this weight is due to excessive eating in the evening and a reluctance to exercise in public because she is dissatisfied with her body/weight.

Elsie has become increasingly socially isolated. She worries that she does not have "smart things to say" at parties and that people will become bored with her. Furthermore, she is self-conscious about her weight and worries that she may be mocked by others. Although she is invited to various social events, she rarely attends. Furthermore, on the rare occasions when she does engage in social interaction, she will often drink three to four glasses of wine immediately before leaving her home. Although she is interested in getting married and having children, she has not dated anyone in over 3 years. Friends will occasionally try to set her up on a date, but she generally refuses to go.

Elsie has recently started Cognitive Behavioral Therapy. While she attends punctually, she often claims that she has "nothing to say" and will do her homework in a cursory fashion, saying that she "wasn't sure how to do it properly."

Case #2

1. What do you imagine are some of the cognitions behind Elsie's lack of social interaction?
2. How would you design a task around attending a party with co-workers, and how could Elsie prepare for this?
3. How would you deal with Elsie's lack of spontaneity in therapy?

4. What role does alcohol play in Elsie's behaviors and how would you address it?

5. How could you begin to help Elsie engage in a healthier and more active lifestyle?

B. Experiential Tasks

1. Describe the key aspects of the cognitive model to your partner as though he or she were a client with anxiety.

2. What will you do to help review/consolidate the skills you have learned over the last several weeks?

3. What are three techniques you could easily incorporate into your practice and try by next week?

4. Set specific homework tasks that use CBT techniques so that you can try to maintain skills or enhance learning.

Quiz

(See Appendix C for answers.)

Please complete the following 25 questions on Cognitive Behavioral Therapy Techniques for Anxiety to the best of your knowledge. Answer as quickly as you can. There is only ONE correct response for each question—choose the best answer to each question.

1. List five cognitive distortions.

    • _____

    • _____

    • _____

    • _____

    • _____

2. List three types of avoidance.

   • _____

   • _____

   • _____

3. Which of the following techniques would be least helpful in working with someone with generalized anxiety disorder?
   a. Cognitive restructuring
   b. Interoceptive exposure
   c. Controlled worry sessions
   d. Automatic Thought Record

4. When assessing someone with physical symptoms of anxiety, all of the following may be significant contributing factors EXCEPT:
   a. Cigarette smoking
   b. Alcohol use
   c. Caffeine intake
   d. The use of benzodiazepines "as needed"

5. Which of the following items would be least appropriate for inclusion on a fear hierarchy?
   a. Going to the mall
   b. Riding the bus
   c. Walking around the block
   d. Going to a friend's house for lunch

6. You are seeing Cindy for CBT treatment of contamination fears in the context of OCD. Which of the following best describes what you would do in an exposure session together?
   a. Touch a doorknob, identify anxiety-related cognitions, and then wash hands
   b. Touch a doorknob, identify anxiety-related cognitions, and then provide reassurance regarding the lack of a real danger
   c. Touch a doorknob, identify anxiety-related cognitions, and then encourage her to touch other "clean" items such as her wallet, purse, and cell phone
   d. Touch a doorknob, identify anxiety-related cognitions, and then practice box breathing

7. You are working on exposure for someone with panic disorder with agoraphobia. While practicing shopping at the supermarket, all of the following may represent "safety behaviors" or subtle forms of avoidance to eventually be targeted in a session EXCEPT:
   a. Pushing a shopping cart
   b. Practicing box breathing
   c. Limiting oneself to purchasing 12 items in order to use the express checkout line
   d. Keeping the mind focused on something else, like a favorite song or poem

The case below applies to questions 8 to 10.
Mr. X is a 42-year-old man with a history of panic disorder. He has become increasingly socially isolated over the last 2 years and is largely confined to

his apartment. He has thoughts like "I'm dying" or "I'm having a heart attack." He refuses to exercise because an increased heart rate seems to trigger his panic attacks.

8. What cognitive distortion is most evident in Mr. X's thinking?
   a. All-or-nothing thinking
   b. Emotional reasoning
   c. Discounting the positive
   d. Catastrophizing

9. Mr. X's refusal to exercise is most in keeping with which of the following?
   a. Avoidance
   b. Interoceptive exposure
   c. Cognitive distortions
   d. Substance abuse

10. Given this clinical scenario, Mr. X is most at risk for developing which condition?
    a. Schizophrenia
    b. Bipolar disorder
    c. Depression
    d. Borderline personality disorder

The case below applies to questions 11 to 13.
Mrs. Z is a 51-year-old executive. She has always been concerned about cleanliness, but in the past year she has begun to wash her hands with

*increasing frequency. She is often late because of the need to sanitize. She
refuses to touch doorknobs or use public bathrooms.*

11. In this case, which of these techniques would be most effective for
    reducing hand washing?
    a. Increased hand-hygiene education
    b. Exposure and response prevention
    c. Activity scheduling
    d. Behavioral activation

12. Which of the following terms describes a recurrent intrusive thought
    about contamination and the need for cleanliness?
    a. A feeling
    b. A parallel process
    c. An obsession
    d. A compulsion

13. A thought record is likely to be of diminished utility in this case
    because:
    a. Thought records never work.
    b. The vast majority of OCD clients appreciate that their
        compulsions are excessive.
    c. The client is unlikely to complete a thought record.
    d. Thought records are only for those who have depression.

14. Emotions are generally:
    a. Intense

b. Uncomfortable

c. Described by a single word

d. Under direct volitional control

15. Thoughts are most associated with:
   a. Behaviors and feelings
   b. Distortions and activities
   c. Exposures
   d. Fear hierarchies

16. With regard to panic attacks, which of the following is INCORRECT?
   a. An individual may be diagnosed with a panic disorder despite having had only a few infrequent panic attacks.
   b. Individuals may be correctly diagnosed with social phobia rather than panic disorder despite having frequent panic attacks.
   c. Symptoms of panic attacks typically linger for several hours.
   d. Thoughts that one is "going crazy" or is going to die are symptoms of a panic attack.

17. All of the following are regarded as first-line treatments for one or more mood/anxiety disorders EXCEPT:
   a. Mindfulness
   b. CBT
   c. IPT
   d. SSRI medication

The case below applies to questions 18 to 20.

You are seeing John, a 47-year-old engineer, regarding his anxiety issues. John describes recurring fears that errors in his work may have catastrophic consequences. As a result he has been having trouble meeting work deadlines over the last year, as he rechecks his work repeatedly. Although he has viewed himself as a worrier since childhood, he viewed his previous worry behavior as reasonable but these recent worries as different and more intrusive. John was feeling down because of these difficulties at times, but he continues so far to function well at home and at work (although he is now slower, he is regarded by his boss and colleagues as a very knowledgeable and dependable member of the team). On further questioning, John also describes "high anxiety attacks" during which he feels suddenly panicky, sweaty, tachycardic, and short of breath, which are typically brought on by particularly severe concerns regarding mistakes he may have made at work.

18. Based on this history, you inform John that the most likely diagnosis is:
    a. A major depressive episode
    b. Obsessive-compulsive disorder
    c. Panic disorder
    d. Generalized anxiety disorder

19. Helpful strategies for treatment of John's condition include all of the following EXCEPT:
    a. Relaxation training
    b. Cognitive restructuring

    c. Exposure and response prevention

    d. Interoceptive exposure

20. After psychoeducation and a discussion of his treatment options, John indicates he would like to try CBT. Which of the following regarding treatment is MOST correct?

    a. John will be expected to practice at weekly therapy sessions.

    b. Exposure sessions tackling triggers identified on John's fear hierarchy can be completed within 15 minutes.

    c. John will benefit most if able to practice challenging his fears daily.

    d. Box breathing is an essential component of John's treatment.

21. You are working with a client on a thought record regarding his fears of "being thought an idiot" and looking like a fool during meetings with his boss. All of the following may be considered "evidence" to be listed in a thought record EXCEPT:

    a. The client's feeling that he will be unable to cope

    b. Previous feedback the client has received that he did well in his last meeting

    c. Symptoms of anxiety the client experiences that he believes others are likely to notice, such as sweating profusely or his hands shaking

    d. Negative feedback the client received in his last job about performing badly in a team meeting

22. Good exposure tasks have all of the following characteristics
    EXCEPT:
    a. Being practical
    b. Being relevant to the client
    c. Requiring extensive preparation to practice
    d. Being collaboratively agreed upon by therapist and client

23. All of the following are true of box breathing EXCEPT:
    a. It involves deliberately slowing down the speed of breathing.
    b. It can be helpful in reducing panic symptoms.
    c. It can be helpful in reducing excessive worry.
    d. It works best if practiced regularly.

24. All of the following are true about interoceptive exposure EXCEPT:
    a. It may result in symptoms of a panic attack.
    b. It can be very anxiety-provoking for clients initially.
    c. It may help clients challenge catastrophic cognitions associated
        with panic symptoms.
    d. It is helpful for symptoms of depression.

25. Mr. Smith is seeing you for CBT to help with his social phobia. You
    review his homework, which was to generate a fear hierarchy, and
    suggest that all of the following are good for inclusion EXCEPT:
    a. Sitting at a table and eating lunch with colleagues
    b. Looking people in the eye at all times
    c. Talking to a cashier at the corner store about the weather
    d. Using urinals in public washrooms

Appendix A:
Role-Play Transcripts

(Refer to the enclosed DVD for the full video.)

I'm Kathy and I'm 40 and for the last year I've been having these episodes. It started at the farmers' market in town. I started getting really dizzy and I couldn't catch my breath and I thought I was having an asthma attack. I was sure I was having an asthma attack, and then my chest got really tight and I started getting hot and sweaty and my arms started tingling and I thought I was going to die. I thought I was going to have a heart attack and die. So my husband took me to the emergency room and they ran all of these tests and they didn't find anything so they sent me home. And it happened again at work a couple of weeks later and again I went to emergency and they didn't find anything. They suggested I come to the mental health clinic and I just thought it would go away on its own and it didn't: It got worse. It got so bad that I had to quit my job and I can't even leave my house on my own anymore. My niece is getting married in 6 months and I really want to be involved in that wedding. I can't live like this anymore.

ROLE PLAY #1: COGNITIVE RESTRUCTURING USING THE AUTOMATIC THOUGHT RECORD

THERAPIST: The last couple of sessions we've been talking a little bit about some of your panic symptoms and a little bit about the cognitive model and I thought today we might try and do a thought record together. Do you think you'd be up for that?

CLIENT: I guess so.

[Identifying a specific situation linked to a change in mood]

T: So we're going to try and fill this thought record out about some situation that's happened in the last week or so. Can you think of any situation where you noticed some change in your mood?

C: Yeah, a couple of days ago I tried to go to the corner store at the gas station for some milk on my own.

T: So in Column #1 let's try and write down the situation. You mentioned it's a couple of days ago, so I guess on Tuesday?

C: Yeah.

[Recording the details of the specific situation]

T: So let's jot that down. And you said you walked into the store.

C: Yeah.

T: Then when is the moment when you first noticed that change in emotion? Is it seeing the store? Is it going in?

c: There were a whole lot more people in there than I was expecting.

t: So that's the moment we're going to try and capture, when you opened the door to the store and you see how many people are there.

c: Okay.

t: About what time of day would you say this was?

c: Ten o'clock, 9:30, 10:00.

[Identifying associated moods or emotions]

t: So let's say around 9:30 or 10:00. You walk to the store, you open up the door, and you see all these people in there. Going on to Column #2, what emotion were you aware of? What did you experience in that moment?

c: I felt like I was going to be in trouble. I felt like . . . I started to panic.

[Differentiating thoughts versus emotions]

t: So you've actually given me two things there. You gave me a thought which we should put in Column #3. You said you felt like you were . . .

c: In trouble.

t: In trouble. So, I'm in trouble, let's put that in Column #3. Then the other thing you mentioned was panic and that sounds like an emotion to me so let's put that in Column #2.

c: Okay.

[Further exploration of associated moods or emotions]

t: Any other emotions that you experienced in that moment when you opened the door?

c: I got really scared.

t: Okay, let's put that down. So you got panicked and scared. Any other emotions?

c: I was worried.

T: And these all sound, in one way or another, connected to anxiety—scared, panicked, worried, so you're consistent. Any other emotions that we missed out on?

C: Not that I can think of offhand.

[Rating intensity of each emotion (0–100%)]

T: So let's rate the emotions that we've got here. We'll use a scale from 0 to 100. Zero is you didn't feel that emotion at all and 100 is the most intensely you've ever felt that before. So, the panic, how high should we rate that?

C: Pretty high—100.

T: What about scared?

C: Maybe a little less but still high—80.

T: And the last one is worried.

C: Sixty.

[Identifying associated automatic thoughts]

T: So, moving on to Column #3, we want to try and capture that moment in time when you're feeling panicked—100, scared—80, and worried—60. What thoughts were going through your head? What were you thinking to yourself?

C: That it was going to happen again.

T: It's going to happen again: let's put that down. What else do you think was going through your head?

C: I thought . . . I started experiencing all of those things and I thought I was going to die.

T: Okay, let's put down, I was going to die.

C: Okay.

T: That's a pretty scary thought. Any other thoughts, maybe about the physical symptoms you were experiencing, what they meant?

C: I guess I started to get a little bit embarrassed.

[Differentiating thoughts versus emotions]

T: And where do you think embarrassed goes? Would that best go in Column #2 or Column #3? Is that a mood or a thought?

C: I guess #2.

T: Okay, so let's put that in Column #2, and that means that we'll have to rate that as well from 0 to 100. How embarrassed do you think you were?

C: Forty, fifty.

T: Should we split the difference?

C: Forty-five, okay.

T: Any other thoughts that you were aware of in that moment when you see all those people?

C: What if I die here and I'm surrounded by strangers?

[Making links between thoughts and feelings]

T: Okay, so let's split that up. One is, what if I die here, we should definitely put that down. And I think a separate but important thought is, I'm surrounded by strangers. And the reason I have broken that up is, you remember in the cognitive model, thoughts and emotions are associated and when I look at the thought, I'm surrounded by strangers, and then I look back at the emotion, embarrassment, that seems to fit. Those two seem to connect.

C: Okay.

T: Any other thoughts that we're missing?

c: Not that I can think of.

[Summarizing]

t: I think you've done a great job. You've got all these anxious emotions and when I look at these thoughts they're pretty anxious-sounding thoughts. I'm in trouble, it's going to happen again, I'm going to die, what if I die here, so there seems to be a connection there between emotions you're experiencing and what's going through your head. Does that make sense so far?

c: Yeah.

[Identifying the "hot thought"]

t: So our next job is to pick one of these thoughts, which we'll call the "hot thought," and that is the thought most driving the emotion. What do you think is the most powerful emotional thought of those ones that you've listed?

c: I'm going to die.

[Exploring evidence that supports the "hot thought"]

t: Let's circle that one. And I agree: that is a powerful and terrifying thought. So, in all the subsequent columns, we're going to be working on that thought in particular.

c: Okay.

t: So in Column #4 we're looking for any evidence that supports that thought that you were going to die. So, remember, evidence is objective; it's provable in a court of law. Have you got any facts like that that might back up the idea that you were going to die in that situation?

c: My chest got tight.

t: So let's put that down. There's no question you experienced some chest tightness.

C: My arms and my hands started to tingle.

T: Okay.

C: I couldn't catch my breath.

T: So those are all objective signs that clearly you experienced that are consistent maybe with dying. Any other evidence that supports the idea that you were going to die in that moment?

C: I got really hot and sweaty.

T: Hot and sweaty, let's put those down. Any others you can think of?

C: I knew that these were all things that prove you're going to have a heart attack, right?

T: So you seem to have some idea that maybe these are symptoms that someone might experience when they're having a heart attack.

C: Uh-huh.

T: Because we're getting evidence now, I'm going to grill you like a lawyer. Where do you have that information from?

C: My mom's friend is a nurse and she told me that these are signs of a heart attack.

T: Okay, so let's put that down. You have from a medical professional some evidence that in fact these are potentially signs of a heart attack. Let's put that down.

C: Okay.

T: Anything else that we are missing?

C: I don't think so.

[Exploring evidence that does not support the "hot thought"]

T: If we come up with anything else, we can always put it in. Let's go on to Column #5. Is there any evidence that supports the opposite, that does not suggest you were going to die in that moment?

C: Besides the fact that I didn't die, I don't know. It's really hard because I've felt that way before and I'm pretty convinced that I'm going to die.

T: Have you had your heart checked at all?

C: Yeah, I've been to the emergency room twice.

T: And what did they tell you there?

C: That my heart was working just fine.

T: They did some tests, something like a cardiogram?

C: They did a whole bunch of tests on my heart, on my lungs, and everything was working fine.

T: That sounds like important evidence. You went and you saw a doctor in the emergency room and they checked out your heart a couple of times and they said your heart was just fine?

C: Uh-huh.

T: Okay, let's put that down. That sounds like very important evidence.

C: Okay.

T: Any other pieces of evidence you can think of that maybe you weren't dying?

C: No.

[Exploring other explanations for appraisal of symptoms]

T: I have one more question for you. You mentioned that you felt sweaty and tingly and your chest was tight. Have you ever had any of these kinds of physical experiences before? Have you ever been sweaty before?

C: Well, yeah, on a hot day I get sweaty.

T: Were you having a heart attack on that occasion?

C: No.

T: Okay, so sometimes we can get sweaty when it's not necessarily a heart attack.

C: Right.

T: Have you ever had tingles in your hands and your feet before?

C: Yeah, I guess so, when I wake up or if they fall asleep sometimes.

T: Yeah, I've had that too. So I think we should put that down as well, that on one hand it's true, that these symptoms are consistent with a heart attack—your nurse friend told you that—but on the other hand, sometimes you can get these symptoms for other reasons and I think that's an important piece of evidence we should capture.

C: Okay.

T: Is that alright?

C: Right.

[Generating an alternative, balanced thought]

T: Okay, let's put that down. So, moving on to Column #6, we are going to try and rewrite that initial hot thought, I'm going to die. That's the terrifying thought that is driving a lot of the anxiety, but this time we're going to try and rewrite it in a way that takes into account all the excellent evidence that you've just generated.

C: Okay.

T: We want to be fair and even-handed. We want you to get some of the stuff from Column #4 and some of the stuff from Column #5 in there, and just as a hint, usually it's an "although" sentence. So something like, although I was sweaty and tingly . . . and then we'd put in some of the other evidence on the other side.

C: So although I thought I was going to die because my chest got tight and my arms were tingling and I couldn't breathe and I knew that

that was evidence that I was going to have a heart attack, I kept breathing and I didn't turn blue and the doctors told me that my heart and lungs were fine.

T: Fabulous. And let's add in that one other big piece of evidence: that you've had these symptoms before and survived them.

C: Right.

T: That's an important one, I think.

C: Yeah.

[Rating strength of belief in the alternative, balanced thought]

T: That's fabulous. So the sentence that you've just created is based only on the evidence that you generated. That's all factual evidence that can't be disputed. The sentence that you just told me, how strongly do you believe it from 0 to 100?

C: Maybe 50.

T: And what do you think prevents you from believing that more?

C: I still feel those symptoms are so real and they are really scary and it's really hard not to believe that maybe somebody is wrong.

T: Okay, I'm glad you don't believe it 100%. That would be suspicious. I think this is the very first time that you're trying one of these exercises and this is a new way of thinking, one that is unfamiliar and, frankly, that you shouldn't trust right away.

C: Okay.

T: So I think that you believing it 50%, that sounds about right. I suspect that if, over time, if you keep practicing these, this new way of thinking might become more believable and you might be able to generate even more and better evidence, but I think for our first try 50% is good.

c: Okay.

[Re-rating emotions (from Column #2) in light of newly generated thought]

t: So let's move on to that last column: this is the payoff column. If you believe that sentence 50%—although you thought you were going to die and you were having those symptoms and you knew they were associated with a heart attack, but also you knew that the doctors had checked you out and you had had them before and you had survived them before—what would you rate the emotions as now? So let's go back to those original emotions. Panic, if you believe this new sentence 50%, where would you rate the panic from 0 to 100?

c: About 50, I guess.

t: Okay, let's put that down. You also mentioned scared.

c: I'm still pretty scared, so maybe that's 50 too.

t: And worried?

c: Thirty.

t: And the last one was embarrassed.

c: Not so embarrassed anymore, maybe 20.

t: For some people they might experience some new emotions. Are there any new emotions we should put in this last column that maybe we didn't capture the first time?

c: I don't think so.

[Concluding and instilling hope]

t: So, Kathy, you've done a fabulous job. You have a lot to be proud of. I want to reinforce to you that this is the first time you've done this exercise and you've already dropped your panic from 100 down to 50. You've dropped your scared from 80 to 50, worried in half from 60 to

30, and your embarrassed dropped by more than half from 45 to 20. And you've done this all just by looking very closely at your thoughts and trying to think about things based on the evidence, a little bit more balanced and a little bit more objectively.

c: Okay.

т: And again, if you keep on doing this and you get better and better at it and it becomes more and more believable, my guess would be you'd get an even bigger drop in some of these anxious symptoms.

c: That sounds good.

ROLE PLAY #2: BOX BREATHING AND INTEROCEPTIVE EXPOSURE

т: Hi, Kathy, it's so good to see you again.

c: Thanks.

т: I know that you've already begun working with Mark on cognitive exercises and I understand you've had some success with that.

c: Yeah.

[Setting the agenda for the session]

т: Which is a wonderful way to start. Today we're going to work on some behavioral techniques that are going to help build on top of that.

c: Okay.

т: What's planned for today are two techniques. One is going to be a method of exposing yourself to anxiety symptoms, bringing them on so that you can learn what they feel like and learn to bring them down again. How does that sound?

C: Not great.

T: It's a tall order.

C: Yeah.

T: Very effective though, and what's going to make it easier is that we are also going to learn a breathing technique that we really use to bring those symptoms down.

C: Okay, that sounds better.

T: It does for most people. So I'd like to try that first, this relaxation breathing technique.

C: Okay.

T: One of the reasons we like this is that, first of all, it's portable, easy, it can be done anywhere. So you can use it for all kinds of things, not specifically limited to when you have panic symptoms. The other thing about it is that it really directly gets at one of the core symptoms of panic, and that is that when you're feeling panicky you're probably breathing a little too rapidly.

C: Okay.

[Exploring client's physical symptoms of anxiety]

T: Have you ever thought about your breathing and what happens when you're anxious?

C: I just can't catch my breath.

T: And what do you think you're doing when you feel that way?

C: I'm more than likely holding my breath because I'm panicking.

T: Right. And then, in response, chances are you're probably breathing a little too quickly.

C: Right.

[Making links between physical symptoms and feelings of anxiety]

T: That's one of the characteristic things that people do, that and breath holding: you're absolutely right. They're both big issues. The problem is that, ironically enough, both those patterns are going to contribute to even more physical symptoms that you then think of as part of your core anxiety symptoms. So we need to identify those and begin to get more familiar and comfortable with them. When people breathe rapidly, they're usually just breathing from their upper chest and not really taking the time to catch their breath.

[Teaching box breathing]

This technique that I'm going to show you is called box breathing. The focus is on taking very deep breaths that use your entire lung capacity. So one of the things that I like to do to start is to have you put your hands on your belly, because if you really breathe using your whole abdomen, your whole chest, you're going to feel your belly move with the breaths.

C: Okay.

T: So if you just breathe normally right now, are your hands moving much?

C: Not much.

T: Typically that's about what most people say. They might get a little bit of movement. So now I'd like to focus on really deep, regular breathing, and we'll talk through it together.

C: Okay.

T: So let's try a deep breath in, completely expanding, and blow it all out. Good. Wait, and again, a deep breath in using all your lung capacity, really feeling the lungs open, and blow it out like a balloon deflating. You'll feel the tension just melt away. A deep breath in and completely let it out again.

c: That feels good.

t: Does it?

c: Yeah.

t: It makes you feel different than before.

c: Yeah.

t: Well, that's wonderful. That's a great start because that means it's a technique that will probably be very useful to you.

c: Okay.

t: We call it a box breathing pattern because, if you think about it, it's kind of like you're breathing in, you're pausing, you're breathing out, you're pausing, so kind of like a box.

c: Okay.

t: So now we have that under our belts and it's going to get better with practice, I should mention as well. Now I'd like to try an exercise that may bring on some of the physical symptoms that you associate with panic.

c: Okay.

t: Why do we want to do this, you might be wondering.

c: Yeah.

t: You're looking anxious as we talk about it.

c: Yeah, I really hate the thought of making myself go there.

[Providing a rationale for interoceptive exposure]

t: Everybody with panic does and part of the problem of course are the anxious thoughts that you have about possible bad things happening, which I know you're already beginning to challenge. The other problem is often the feeling that these symptoms are just beyond your control, and the purpose, the beauty, of this exercise is that if we bring on symptoms that for you feel fairly panic-like and then can use our breathing to reduce them, it gives you a whole different perspective on whether or not these symptoms are manageable.

c: Okay.

T: Doesn't it?

c: Yeah.

T: Do you feel willing to try it with me here?

c: Yeah.

[Preparing the client to anticipate anxiety symptoms from rapid breathing]

T: So the exercise I'd like to do with you today is what we call rapid breathing or hyperventilation, the reason being, as we discussed for you, partly you hold your breath but partly you may be breathing too rapidly in response to anxiety as well. And people vary. Some people will get very little in the way of symptoms; for others it might come on quite quickly and bring on a number of the symptoms you talked about, things like feeling spacey or light-headed. And I have to tell you, it happens usually right away for me. I'm quite sensitive to this. After a while you may notice some of the tingling or other funny sensations you've mentioned, or numbness, or even some of the faintness you've experienced. So let's try it together until we seem to have a number of these symptoms, if it works, and then we're going to go from that to our box breathing.

c: Okay.

T: Okay, so let's give it a shot. We're going to pant shallowly just like a dog on a hot summer day.

C: Okay.

T: I can tell you I'm already getting a little spacey. How are you?

C: I don't like this very much.

[Identifying and encouraging tolerance of anxiety symptoms]

T: Is it bringing on any symptoms? What are you feeling so far?

C: I'm starting to feel really dizzy.

T: Good, excellent. Let's see what else comes up. The difference is, now we are looking for these things.

C: I'm getting sweaty.

T: Good, can you go another moment? Try and keep it up a little longer. Any other symptoms?

C: My hands are starting to tingle.

[Making links to panic attacks]

T: Excellent. So you've got some dizziness, some sweatiness, some tingling, a number of the symptoms. Do they feel like you get in a panic attack?

C: Yeah.

[Using box breathing to reduce anxiety]

T: That's a great start then. This is a great thing today. So now I'd like you to make sure your hands are down low and let's focus on doing the box breathing again.

C: Okay.

[Checking in to re-rate symptoms]

T: Deep breath all the way in, fully expanding, pause, and blow it all out. Relax and let it go. Deep breath in and blow it all out. Let the tension melt away as you do that. Relax into it. One last time, deep breath in and let it all go. How are you feeling now?

C: Better.

T: Are the symptoms still there?

C: No.

T: Not at all?

C: They're pretty much gone.

[Encouraging client to reappraise her capacity to cope with anxiety symptoms]

T: That's wonderful. So what does that tell you about being able to manage these symptoms? Do you think it's something you could do in the future?

C: I'll definitely give it a try.

[Linking cognitive reappraisal and potential for decreased anxiety]

T: Do you think it would change your feelings of anxiety knowing that you might be able to bring the symptoms down?

C: I think it might.

T: That's terrific. That's a great start. You can always use this when you need it.

C: Okay.

T: So I'm going to want you to practice that and we'll talk about more techniques the next time I see you.

C: Thanks.

ROLE PLAY #3: CREATING A FEAR
HIERARCHY FOR GRADED EXPOSURE

T: So now we want to finish off today with the last of the really big key
    techniques that we need to start working on.

C: Okay.

T: And that is actually beginning to practice getting you back into situa-
    tions you've been avoiding.

C: Okay.

T: Really, that's where the payoff is. So what we're going to do today is
    develop a hierarchy and a hierarchy is a list of situations that bring
    on your anxiety right now. So these can be situations that you either
    avoid completely, and some of them will be the tough things that you
    know about, that are really reliable triggers for you. And then at the
    other end there may be some situations which you still enter, you still
    do regularly, but you dislike it because they bring on some symptoms
    although they're milder and more manageable.

C: Okay.

T: Okay, we're going to want to generate a list of maybe 5 to 15 of these
    kinds of triggers or situations for you and begin to plan out how we're
    going to approach your anxiety symptoms.

C: Okay.

T: So we have here a copy of a list and this is going to be for your hier-
    archy. Let's each take a pen and we're going to do this together. The
    idea then is to generate a list of situations. We want them to be really
    specific so that we both understand exactly what the situation is. It's
    also important that they be something practical. It's got to involve

a place or an area that you can get to readily on your own because you're going to need to be practicing this pretty frequently.

C: Okay.

T: A rough rule of thumb is practicing at least three times a week and the more you practice, of course, the better you get at developing your new skills. So let's give a stab at trying to come up with some of these triggers. Right now we don't need to worry about the order but when we move forward with it we'll plan that order very carefully, beginning with things that are easy and gradually moving up to the hard ones.

C: Okay.

T: Does that sound okay?

C: Yeah, that sounds great.

[Identifying specific, anxiety-producing, avoided situations]

T: So what would be an example of a situation right now that brings on anxiety that you might avoid because of it?

C: I never go to the corner store, the gas station, anymore.

T: And those are important things on a practical, day-to-day perspective, aren't they?

C: Yeah.

[Beginning to list and rate feared activities]

T: Okay, so let's write, going to the corner store. Let's also write, going to the gas station.

C: They're the same.

T: Okay, if they're the same we don't need them both. How much would you say you fear going to the corner store and the gas station if you had to rate it from 0 to 100?

C: That's 100.

T: So this is a very difficult one: that's great. What are some other situations that you've not been comfortable in?

C: I don't like walking out to the end of the lane to get the mail or the paper.

T: Excellent example. How far is it to the end of your lane?

C: It's quite a ways, quite a ways from the farmhouse, so maybe a 5-minute walk.

T: Can you still see the farmhouse when you're there?

C: Yeah, but I know I'm not close.

T: So what should we write here, going to get the mail?

C: Yeah.

T: That's a really good one, and again, probably something you want to be doing most days.

C: Yeah.

T: How much anxiety would you say you have in that situation now?

C: Thirty, forty.

T: So we'll say 35. So it's one that makes you distinctly uncomfortable but it's still kind of manageable.

C: Maybe, yeah. I don't think I'm going to bump into anybody. The road is busy but there won't be a whole lot of people so I think I could probably . . . maybe it's a little higher than 35, now that we're talking about it. Maybe it's closer to . . . the road is pretty busy, so 50.

T: Sure, the point of this is that it's never written in stone. We can always change it as we go along.

C: Okay.

T: We can always change the order of things or even the specific items themselves.

c: Okay.

t: The idea is to make it work for you.

c: Okay.

t: So we're off to a really good start here. We've got going to the corner store and going to the mailbox.

c: Yeah.

t: And we've rated those as 100 and 50, respectively.

c: Yeah.

[Helping to identify other avoided situations]

t: I'm wondering, though, because I think you mentioned going to the market being a very difficult situation for you.

c: In town, yeah, yeah.

t: Is that an important place for you to be able to get to?

c: There's no way I would go there now.

t: Do you need to be able to get there if you were well?

c: Yeah.

t: So how bad would that be?

c: That's 100, without question.

t: So I'm going to write, going to the market and I'm putting that at 100%. But we had going to the corner store at 100% before so do you think that maybe that needs to change a little?

c: Yeah, that's not quite as bad, maybe 80.

t: Okay, 80% then. So that will often happen. Sometimes as we fill in we'll realize we need to shift things around a little and that's perfect.

c: Okay.

[Identifying situations that produce minimal anxiety on the fear hierarchy]

T: So we've got a number of things now and this is looking really good. We've got a very tough one and an important thing: being able to get to the market. We've got going to the corner store, going to your mailbox, but all of these are fairly challenging right now. What would be something a little easier that you could think of?

C: Maybe sitting on my front veranda on my own.

T: Do you do that currently?

C: Not on my own.

T: Not on your own at all?

C: No.

T: How much anxiety would be associated with doing it on your own now?

C: Maybe 10.

T: So it's something that's not going to produce a lot of anxiety but you've been avoiding anyway.

C: Yeah.

T: So let's put that down, sitting on veranda. Ten is a really low rating. I wonder if we could think of something just a little more challenging than that, maybe in the 25 to 30, 35% range, perhaps a little further from home.

C: Definitely, going to hang out the clothes or doing the gardening on my own.

T: Those both sound like good examples. Why don't we go with perhaps being in your garden?

C: Okay.

T: Because another thing to keep in mind is that when you start working on these things you're going to need to stay in these situations until the anxiety abates and that may take time. So sitting in the garden would be an easy way to pass the time probably, or gardening for that matter.

c: Okay.

t: So I'm going to write, gardening, and how much anxiety do you think you'd have in that situation now?

c: Twenty-five or 30. It's quite a ways from the farmhouse so . . .

t: So this is really good work, Kathy. We have a list of a number of things already spanning from 10% fear or anxiety with sitting on the veranda, which is probably something really pretty easy for you even though you haven't been doing it, right up to going to the market, which is really the toughest situation right now that you could think of at 100.

c: Yeah.

t: And what we're going to begin doing is getting you to practice, starting with an easy one, on a regular basis. And as you get better, more skilled at dealing with them and having less anxiety in these situations, you'll gradually find that going up your hierarchy to the next situation is not going to seem like such a big step.

c: Okay.

[Planning practicalities of exposure on the fear hierarchy]

t: So they all get much more manageable and as we move up, the one that right now you rated as 100 is no longer going to be 100. It's going to feel a lot more manageable when you get there. This week, I'm wondering, it seems to me that sitting on the veranda is probably very easy, or what do you think? You tell me.

c: I think I could probably do it.

T: I think so too, so I'm wondering, we could start with that one or we could make it a little more of a challenge and say starting to sit in the garden. Or we could even compromise. Maybe you could put a chair somewhere below the veranda on the near edge of the garden. How would that work?

C: I can try that.

T: What do you think that would be like?

C: I guess somewhere in between. I think I can try it though.

T: Do you feel confident about that one?

C: Yes.

T: Perfect, so maybe around a 20, perhaps?

C: Yeah.

T: That would be a great starting point and the idea is going to be to spend time sitting there until the anxiety comes down. You can use your box breathing if it's helpful and gradually we're going to build up your confidence in doing these things again.

C: Okay.

Appendix B:
Practice Reminder Summary

(Refer to the enclosed Practice Reminder Card.)

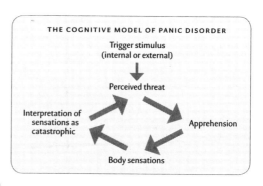

THE COGNITIVE MODEL OF PANIC DISORDER

Trigger stimulus
(internal or external)

Perceived threat

Interpretation of
sensations as
catastrophic

Apprehension

Body sensations

FEELINGS ARE LINKED TO
THOUGHTS AND BEHAVIORS

Use both cognitive and behavioral techniques:

1. **Psychoeducation**

2. **Cognitive restructuring**: Use the Automatic Thought Record to minimize the sense of danger and increase the sense of self-efficacy.

3. **Interoceptive exposure** can help clients to be less afraid of symptoms.

4. Graded behavioral exposure by using a **fear hierarchy** helps clients to disconfirm their fears and confirm their capacity to cope.

KEY POINTS OF CBT

1. Just because you think something doesn't necessarily mean that it is true.
2. CBT helps clients think realistically in a balanced way.
3. Thoughts can be examined cognitively *or* tested behaviorally.
4. New behaviors can serve to alter thoughts or gather facts.
5. How you think about events is more important than the events themselves.

Use Socratic Questioning and Guided Discovery

- What would happen if this were true?
- How likely do you think this is?
- What would you say to a friend in the same situation?

WHAT DO YOU FEAR WILL HAPPEN?

Panic Disorder
I will have a panic attack.
I will be unable to escape or function.
I will die from my anxiety.

Social Phobia
I will embarrass myself.
I will be humiliated.
I will fail under scrutiny.

Generalized Anxiety Disorder
Recurrent and intrusive worries that something realistically bad could happen to me or my family such as:
  Death/illness
  Financial problems
  All my worrying will kill me

Obsessive Compulsive Disorder (OCD)
Intrusive thoughts that something very bad will happen and it will be my fault:
The door is left unlocked . . . and will result in a break-in.
The stove is left on . . . and will start a fire.
If I touch anything dirty, . . . I'll get sick or make others sick.
I'll think bad thoughts . . . and they will come true.
If I don't [get up from a chair, close a door, step on a crack] just right, . . . something bad will happen.

PSYCHOEDUCATION

Lifestyle advice and nondrug strategies:

- Lifestyle advice:
  - Decrease any excessive use of caffeine, alcohol, nicotine, and chocolate

- Minimize the use of sedatives/hypnotics
- Get a good night's sleep
- Get regular aerobic exercise
- Use relaxation/breathing retraining.
- Panic attacks are not life-threatening.
- CBT is likely to be helpful in reducing distress.

COGNITIVE RESTRUCTURING: AUTOMATIC THOUGHT RECORD:

Ask the client, "What was going through your mind just then? What do you think you were thinking about? What did the situation mean to you (or mean about you)?"

COLUMN #1: Identify a specific moment in time and situation when the client noticed some change in emotion.

COLUMN #2: List any emotions that the client was feeling in the situation described in Column #1, and have the client rate the intensity of those moods from 0 to 100.

COLUMN #3: Capture the automatic thoughts that spontaneously come unbidden to the client's mind in that moment when the client experienced a specific change in emotion. Then identify the "hot thought" that is most driving the emotion.

COLUMN #4: List evidence that supports the hot thought, and in Column #5 list evidence that does not support the hot thought.

COLUMN #6: Collaboratively rewrite the hot thought in a fashion that is based on the evidence that was generated. This alternative evidence-based thought stands in opposition to the automatic thought that came from the client's biases based on his or her own ways of thinking and prior experiences.

COLUMN #7: Ask the client to re-rate the intensity of the moods that are listed in Column #2. If all has gone well, there should be a decrease in some of the negative emotions, as a result of a more balanced way of thinking.

Use the Downward Arrow Technique to identify further thoughts and enhance understanding by asking, "If this were true, what does that mean?" or "If this were true, what does that say about you?"

Encourage clients to use diaries and self-ratings of symptoms (including duration, anxiety severity [0–100], and physical symptoms), cognitions (automatic thoughts), rituals, and homework.

INTEROCEPTIVE EXPOSURE

Learning to become less frightened by internal symptoms

Technique	*Associated Symptoms*
• Run in place for 1 min.	• Fast heart rate
• Spin in chair for 1 min.	• Dizziness
• Hyperventilate for 1 min.	• Light-headedness, numbness, blurred vision
• Breathe through a straw for 2 mins. with nose plugged	• Shortness of breath

Moving From the Cognitive to the Behavioral

Target avoidance with exposure and box breathing.

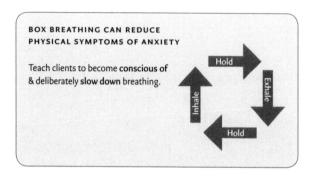

BOX BREATHING CAN REDUCE PHYSICAL SYMPTOMS OF ANXIETY

Teach clients to become **conscious of** & deliberately **slow down** breathing.

Hold
Inhale
Exhale
Hold

Exposure Using a Fear Hierarchy

List **specific** anxiety-producing activities and rate them in an ascending order of difficulty.

- Plan practicalities of exposure, starting with the easiest in an ascending order of difficulty.
  - Practice at least three times a week, staying in the activity until the anxiety subsides (~ 1 hour).
  - The more often and the longer the exposure, the better!
- Rate Anxiety/Avoidance before and after exposure (0–100).
- Anticipate and discuss obstacles.

Appendix C: Answer Key

A. **Discussion**

1. The information in Column #1 highlights a specific moment in time when there was a mood shift. The more specific the information is, the more it will facilitate the identification of hot thoughts. Specific information helps the client to better access thoughts and emotions by putting him or her back in that particular moment.

2. Suicidality is a thought.

3. This is an important distinction because we cannot affect our emotions directly, so if suicidality is a feeling, we're stuck. However, if a person is thinking about suicide, there may be other ways to think and cognitive techniques may be applied.

4. The hot thought is the thought that is most strongly associated with the change in emotion. The hot thought is identified by using the Downward Arrow Technique and by visualizing the situation in detail to enhance memory and affect.

5. Having a framework to understand emotions as opposed to considering them as unexplained phenomena can be reassuring. On the other hand, it is sometimes distressing, depressing, or embarrassing to be in touch with our thoughts.

6. Automatic thoughts are generated spontaneously in given situations based on our underlying beliefs and assumptions.

7. Thoughts are ideas that may or may not be true, generally stemming from previous experience. Evidence is objective and factual.

8. We collect "evidence for" in order to create a believable, balanced alternative thought.

9. Core beliefs develop, often at a young age, through previous experiences.

LESSON PLAN #2

A. Discussion

1. Box breathing works by focusing on slowing down breathing, which helps to reduce the heart rate and other "fight or flight" responses and which minimizes the physical symptoms of anxiety.

2. Progressive muscle relaxation and visual imagery are relaxation techniques. If clients rely too heavily on these coping techniques,

they can become crutches and develop into forms of avoidance, generally known as safety behaviors.

3. Spinning in a circle, breathing into a bag, blowing through a straw, and running up and down stairs are methods to generate interoceptive exposure.

4. The two main rules of exposure are (1) the more often, the better, and (2) the longer it lasts, the better.

5. It is okay if your client develops a panic attack during exposure and sometimes it is even desirable. The idea of exposure is that the client learns that she can experience the physical symptoms but still survive them.

6. Using medications "as needed" to relieve anxiety is contraindicated in CBT. It sends the message that anxiety is dangerous rather than the message that anxiety is uncomfortable but will ultimately pass.

7. Alcohol works similarly to benzodiazepines in that it dampens anxiety; as such, its use is discouraged as these exercises are intended to expose the client to the feared sensations.

8. The physical sensations of anxiety are associated with danger such as illness or death. Furthermore, anxious people generally do not believe that they can cope with these physical sensations.

9. At the end of the exposure, emphasize that anxiety is time-limited, clients are able to cope with more than they initially believed, and that the symptoms can be brought on through normal activities.

LESSON PLAN #3

A. Discussion

1. Clients will generally rate their anxiety and degree of avoidance on scales from 0 to 100.

2. If the steps on a hierarchy are too steep, the client is likely to encounter more anxiety than he can tolerate. The idea is to slowly increase the difficulty over time.

3. Be creative—for something like riding public transportation, you might vary the time of day, whether the client is accompanied or alone, the length of the trip, the area of town through which the vehicle travels, the day of the week, the location on the vehicle, etc.

4. Behavioral exposures are ultimately meant to help clients gain experience and data with respect to situations that are perceived to be threatening. In order to do this effectively, clients must make a prediction in advance and then determine the extent to which the exposure confirms or disconfirms the prediction.

5. Starting at the top of the hierarchy is known as "flooding." It can be done and is highly effective. However, the vast majority of anxious clients will be unwilling to engage in this extreme type of exposure. The hierarchy allows them to slowly move toward increasingly challenging exposures.

6. SUDS stands for "subjective unit of distress score." It is a client rating that is generally rated from 0 to 100.

7. The longer the client spends on exposure, the better, but it should be at least as long as it takes to reduce their anxiety to below a SUDS of 40 or half of the peak, whichever is higher.

8. Signs that a client is ready to move on to the next exposure task include the client saying things like "this is easy" or "I'm bored." Alternatively you can move on when the peak of anxiety is routinely lower than when the exposure was initially attempted.

9. Thought records can be used, even in the midst of an exposure, to help balance out anxious thoughts.

10. There is no such thing as failure in CBT. Experiments that do not proceed as planned still yield important information about areas of difficulty that can be used as fodder for a future thought record or to refine the behavioral task for the next attempt.

LESSON PLAN #4

A. Discussion

Case #1

1. Chloe might be thinking "I'm dying," "I'm having a heart attack," "I can't cope," "If I'm seen, I'll be criticized," or "My symptoms are obvious to others."

2. Coach Chloe to minimize avoidance, to consider having a discussion with her manager, or to consider a transfer to a different department.

3. The advantages of an as-needed anxiolytic are that Chloe will feel less anxiety, she may have a better sense of being able to cope, and it may enhance the therapeutic alliance. The disadvantages are that she could become addicted to benzodiazepines, she may experience "rebound anxiety" due to withdrawal, and there may be memory impairment and a greater risk of falls. Further-

more, Chloe may attribute success to medication rather than to her increasing sense of being able to cope.

4.   Chloe could speak with her boss's supervisor, review her previous performance evaluations, take an assertiveness course, set firm boundaries with her boss in terms of acceptable tone and language, request feedback be given in a more private setting, and complete thought records.

5.   Advertising is about shaping people's ideas. To borrow from CBT, it's not the situation that counts, it's how you think about it. Advertising is all about promoting certain patterns of thinking in an effort to increase awareness and profit. Adopting this attitude may give Chloe some relief.

Case #2

1.   Elsie may be thinking "I have nothing interesting to say," "I'm boring," "Nobody wants to talk to me," "I'll embarrass myself," or "I can't cope."

2.   You would work through a plan in explicit detail, encouraging Elsie to interact with her co-workers. You might rehearse and prepare specific topics of conversation, ask Elsie to make a prediction about how things will go before she attends, and ask her to rate her anxiety during the party to see if her predictions were accurate.

3.   Address Elsie's lack of spontaneity empathically but directly. Have her make a list of the advantages and disadvantages of engaging in therapy, and ask her to create a thought record to explore her thoughts and feelings in therapy.

4. Elsie is using alcohol as an avoidance tool. It must be eliminated in order for her to truly be exposed to the social situation, survive it, and learn from the experience. This can be discussed in therapy with psychoeducation provided. A separate addictions program might be warranted depending on the extent of her use.

5. Have Elsie record the advantages and disadvantages of working out. Get her to gradually expose herself to working out by finding out what kinds of physical activities she prefers; establish a hierarchy that likely will involve some imaginal exposure, followed by going to the place where she plans to work out and gradually increasing the time and intensity of exposure.

QUIZ

1. List five cognitive distortions.
    - All-or-nothing thinking
    - Overgeneralization
    - Mental filter
    - Discounting the positive
    - Jumping to conclusions
    - Magnification
    - Emotional reasoning
    - "Should" statements
    - Labeling
    - Personalization

2. List three types of avoidance.
    - Alcohol ingestion
    - Benzodiazepine use

- Other drug use
- Leaving a situation
- Trying not to think about a situation
- Isolating at home
- Compulsive behaviors
- Excessive unproductive worry

3. b. Interoceptive exposure is a technique specifically helpful for clients who are made more anxious by their somatic anxiety symptoms, typically those individuals for whom panic attacks are a major focus of their difficulty.

4. a. Alcohol and benzodiazepine withdrawal may bring on somatic anxiety symptoms, as does caffeine use. Nicotine levels do not normally have a significant impact on anxiety.

5. d. While a to c are all items that could be practiced as often as the client wishes, (d) would depend on being able to make appropriate plans and, as such, would not necessarily be something practical to practice several times per week.

6. c. Both the ritual (in a) and reassurance (in b) tend to maintain the fear cycle in OCD. Box breathing (as in d) may be helpful for anxiety symptoms but is not necessary for effective treatment. However, dealing with associated avoidance and safety behaviors (as in c) is critically helpful.

7. b. Behaviors identified in a, c, and d all represent safety behaviors, limiting the effectiveness of the exposure—pushing a shopping cart may be used by clients fearful of dizziness or fainting, and distraction limits usefulness of exposure.

8. d. Catastrophizing

9. a. Avoidance

10. c. Depression

11. b. Exposure and response prevention

12. c. An obsession

13. b. The vast majority of OCD clients appreciate that their compulsions are excessive.

14. c. Described by a single word

15. a. Behaviors and feelings

16. c. Panic disorder may be diagnosed in an individual with as few as two reported panic attacks, if they meet criteria for ongoing worry or change in behavior as a result of the attacks. However, panic attacks are nonspecific and may occur regularly in other anxiety disorders, that is, in relation to fear-provoking social interactions in the case of someone with social phobia. Attacks typically resolve within 1 hour.

17. a. While there is evidence of the utility of mindfulness in combination with CBT, it has not been shown to be an effective first-line treatment when delivered as a monotherapy.

18. b. John's primary complaint suggests intrusive fears and associated checking rituals, which are consistent with OCD and unlike the worries of GAD, which are typically viewed as "reasonable," although excessive. Although his history is suggestive of panic attacks, these seem to occur in the context of obsessions rather than "out of the blue" as in panic disorder. His complaint of a low mood is unlikely to meet the severity threshold for a diagnosis of a major depressive episode as he still functions well.

19. a. Relaxation training is not considered an essential component

of CBT, although some individuals may find it helpful in managing anxiety.

20. c. ERP is most effective for treatment of OCD if practiced at least five times weekly, ideally daily. Exposure sessions need to be long enough for the fear to habituate to be maximally helpful, which typically requires up to 1 hour. Although box breathing may be helpful for managing panic symptoms, it is not essential for a good treatment outcome.

21. a. Feelings do not constitute evidence for a thought record!

22. c. Good exposure tasks require some preparation in order to set them up properly, but this preparation is rarely intensive and often can be coordinated in a fairly short period of time.

23. c. Box breathing involves slow, deep, deliberate breathing and is a useful relaxation technique that may also reduce symptoms of panic attacks, particularly if related to hyperventilation. However, it will not address or reduce excessive worry directly. Like all CBT techniques, it works best if practiced regularly.

24. d. Interoceptive exposure is a technique used exclusively for the treatment of somatic anxiety symptoms. It involves the intentional production of physical symptoms associated with anxiety so that clients can challenge their catastrophic beliefs about them and learn from the experience.

25. b. Making eye contact may be a very important task for someone with social anxiety, but for the hierarchy the task must be laid out more specifically, that is, making eye contact with colleagues during hallway conversations. Commencing a new task and attempting to practice it at every opportunity throughout the day immediately may be overwhelming.

References

Beck, A. T. (2005). The current state of cognitive therapy: A 40-year retrospective. *Archives of General Psychiatry, 62*(9), 953–959.

Beck, A. T., & Hurvich, M. S. (1959). Psychological correlates of depression: Frequency of "masochistic" dream content in a private practice sample. *Psychosomatic Medicine, 21*(1), 50–55.

Beck, A. T., Rush, A. J., Shaw, B. F., & Emery, G. (1979). *Cognitive therapy of depression.* New York, NY: Guilford Press.

Clark, D. M. (1986). A cognitive approach to panic. *Behavior Research and Therapy, 24*(4), 461–470.

Clark, D. M., Salkovskis, P. M., Hackman, A., Middleton, H., Anastasiades, P., & Gelder, M. (1994). A comparison of cognitive therapy, applied relaxation and imipramine in the treatment of panic disorder. *British Journal of Psychiatry, 164*(6), 759–769.

Greenberger, D., & Padesky, C. A. (1995). *Mind over mood: Changing the way you feel by changing the way you think.* New York, NY: Guilford Press.

Hawton, K., Salkovskis, P. M., Kirk, J., & Clark, D. M. (1989). *Cognitive behavior therapy for psychiatric problems: A practical guide.* Oxford, UK: Oxford University Press.

Leahy, R. (2005). *The worry cure: Seven steps to stop worry from stopping you.* New York, NY: Three Rivers Press.

Ravitz, P., Cooke, R. G., Mitchell, S., Reeves, S., Teshima, J., Lokuge, B., . . . Zaretsky, A. (2013). Continuing education to go: Capacity-building in psychotherapies for front-line mental health workers in underserviced communities. *Canadian Journal of Psychiatry, 58* (6).

Roshanaei-Moghaddam, B., Pauly, M. C., Atkins, D. C., Baldwin, S. A., Stein, M. B., & Roy-Byrne, P. (2011). Relative effects of CBT and pharmacotherapy in depression versus anxiety: Is medication somewhat better for depression, and CBT somewhat better for anxiety? *Depression & Anxiety, 28*(7), 560–567.

Stanley, M. A., Beck, J. G., & Glassco, J. D. (1996). Treatment of generalized anxiety in older adults: A preliminary comparison of cognitive-behavioral and supportive approaches. *Behavior Therapy, 27,* 565–581.